Masters of the Crafts

Masters of the Crafts

Recipients of the
Saidye Bronfman Award
for Excellence
in the Crafts, 1977–86

Canadian Museum
of Civilization

Research for the book and the exhibition was carried out by Stephen Inglis, who also oversaw the writing of the text.

Harry Foster, chief photographer of the Canadian Museum of Civilization, photographed the works of craft.

DSS catalogue no. NM98-3/56-1989E
Printed and bound in Canada

Published by the
Canadian Museum of Civilization
100 Laurier Street
P.O. Box 3100, Station B
Hull, Quebec
J8X 4H2

Édition française
De main de maître: Les lauréats du Prix d'Excellence en Artisanat Saidye Bronfman, 1977–1986
ISBN 0-660-90289-3
Publié par le Musée canadien des civilisations

Canadian Cataloguing in Publication Data

Main entry under title:
Masters of the crafts: recipients of the Saidye Bronfman Award for Excellence in the Crafts, 1977–86

Issued also in French under title: De main de maître.

Bibliography: p.

ISBN 0-660-10788-0

1. Handicraft – Canada – Awards. 2. Artisans – Canada – Awards. 3. Art – Canada – Awards. 4. Bronfman family – Art patronage. I. Canadian Museum of Civilization. II. Title: Recipients of the Saidye Bronfman Award for Excellence in the Crafts, 1977–86.

NK841.M37 1989   745.5'07'9   C89-097085-8

Contents

Acknowledgements

The tenth anniversary of the Saidye Bronfman Award for Excellence in the Crafts set in motion the chain of events that led to the publication of this book. The new collection of fine crafts it introduces and the exhibition it complements were made possible by the support and assistance of the Samuel and Saidye Bronfman Family Foundation and the Canadian Crafts Council. This museum is grateful to the officers and staffs of these organizations, in particular John Hobday of the Foundation and Peter Weinrich of the Crafts Council.

The artists shared their time, their memories and some of their works to enrich this book and the exhibition. Not only did they donate or lend works but, in providing information on the materials, processes and techniques of their crafts, they have added immeasurably to the Museum's archival resources.

Many others have given of their time and expertise. The members of the Selection Committee that chose the works acquired for the collection included Hugh Hamilton, Stephen Inglis, Leslie Manning, Patricia McClelland, Ann Mortimer, and Peter Weinrich. Important donations to the collection were made by Ann Mortimer and Pierre Berton, to whom the Museum would like to express particular thanks.

The exhibition also benefited from the generosity of many lenders, namely Mr. and Mrs. Charles Bronfman, M. Joan Chalmers, Sharon Schwartz, Ann Mortimer, External Affairs Canada, the Musée du Québec, the National Museum of Natural Sciences, the Ontario Crafts Council, the Royal British Columbia Museum, and the Museum of Anthropology, University of British Columbia.

Foreword

by George F. MacDonald

The sweeping curves of its new building offer the Canadian Museum of Civilization a dynamic exhibition space and an opportunity to help shape a new era. The forces at work in modern Canada – internationalism, multiculturalism, and high-tech communication – suggest exciting directions for museums.

One is toward diversity in collections and the ways in which they are presented to the public. The old categories by which museums separate and classify artifacts according to status labels like civilized versus primitive, fine versus folk, or art versus craft are being replaced by an approach that seeks to show interconnections rather than distinctions between social groups and their forms of cultural expression.

Another direction is toward the study and presentation of process rather than simply the finished product. This has profound implications for museums as they turn more toward concerns of the present and future rather than only those of the past. By involving artists in their programmes, museums will enable visitors to better understand and even share in the creative process. In a society changing as quickly as that of Canada's, this is one way that cultural institutions can adapt their programmes to the changing needs and interests of the community.

It is appropriate that the Museum of Civilization should be publishing this book to coincide with the opening of its new building and the exhibition "Masters of the Crafts". Through the work of outstanding artists like these we can link the qualities of craftsmanship displayed by the oldest artifacts in our collections with those shown by modern works of art. The traditional and enduring concern of craftspeople with materials and processes enables us to share with visitors some of the mystery of making things.

The master craftspeople featured in this book were recipients of the Saidye Bronfman Award for Excellence in the Crafts during its first decade. Together they exemplify the wide range of skills, backgrounds and ideas that have brought vitality to this stream of the arts in Canada.

First, I wish to acknowledge the contribution of the artists themselves, who gave of their time, energy and insight to make this book and the exhibition possible.

We are extremely grateful to the Samuel and Saidye Bronfman Family Foundation for providing the financial support to acquire a collection of works from the featured artists, to conduct the research, mount the exhibition and produce this book. It is in part due to the

Foundation's longstanding sponsorship of the crafts and its support for this particular project that there will be a gallery devoted to fine crafts in the new museum.

The Canadian Crafts Council, which administers the Award, has also been a strong supporter of the Museum of Civilization and has generously assisted in every phase of the project. In addition to offering their own resources and expertise, members of the Council have acted as a link between the Museum and the donors, lenders to the exhibition, and specialists in the crafts field.

One challenge of the new era that all Canadians face is the need to share, to join forces to understand each other in a more profound way. For museums, this involves co-ventures with associations, agencies and specialists of all kinds, rather than striking out alone. This project exemplifies that kind of cooperative effort, and we now invite readers and visitors to enjoy the results.

Introduction:
A Very Short History of Craft

by Peter Weinrich

The Distant Past

Some early crafts were "mysteries", that is, more or less sacred rites with mysterious happenings at their centre, carried out by people with special gifts – and the grace of the gods. The art of the blacksmith was a "black art" in more than one sense, and the smelting of ore from Mother Earth involved a mysterious transformation. Myths have grown up around such arts in many countries.

The earliest civilizations demonstrate a clear distinction between simple utilitarian objects – clay bowls and pitchers, carrying baskets, storage boxes – and objects of great luxury and refinement for use in palace and temple – crowns, reliquaries, shrines. This distinction is still with us. Monarchies and religions have declined in influence, but luxury is far from dead. We may regret the lack of ceremony and sacrament, public and private, but we still have chains of office, the Speaker's mace, and medals of honour. Luxury today often includes objects declared to be "art", that is, unique works with a purely aesthetic function.

Traditionally, in most societies, craft techniques were taught to apprentices or simply passed down from father to son, mother to daughter. Many of the makers of works for sacrament and ceremony formed tightly knit groups of family or clan, which later developed into the well-known guilds of medieval times. But over the centuries the era when city air meant freedom from rural bondage passed, and free-spirited craftsmen made their way outside the sway of the city-bound guilds. The guilds that remained became stultified closed shops. The industrial revolution sealed their fate; the guilds transformed themselves into craft-based trade unions, or became backwaters of pomp, livery, tradition, gold watch chains and annual dinners. Traditional craftsmanship, such as it was, lingered on as a cottage industry or was placed in the service of the machine: cutting cog-wheels, forging new tools or making elaborate moulds. Not until the revolts of Ruskin, Morris, the Jugenstil and the Sezession did the picture begin to change.

Apart from objects for sacrament and ceremony, much of what we now call crafts meant essentially utilitarian objects that were a pleasure to handle and possess: they did more than simply fulfil a useful purpose. In David Pye's words,* they had been subjected to "useless

*David Pye, *The Nature of Design* (London: Studio Vista, 1964), 9–10.

work", meaning work that was unnecessary for their efficient functioning – fine polishing, for example, and decoration of all kinds. Of course, the human body itself has always been regarded as an object to be decorated, whether with jewellery, tattooing, scarification or woad. Alas, the late-Victorian penchant for overloading every object with curlicues, strapwork, rosebuds and acanthus leaves, derived from every conceivable historical period, brought the decorative arts into disrepute; they became the *over-decorated* arts. But we do well to remember that many of the greatest artists of earlier epochs, the Renaissance for example, did not hesitate to turn their skills to the design of costumes, scenery, goblets, tapestries and triumphal arches. In fact, many of them, like Ghiberti, Verrocchio, Botticelli and Brunelleschi, actually trained in the guild of goldsmiths.

The Recent Past

The 1960s and early 1970s saw a great increase in people producing crafts for a livelihood, professionals in fact. These were the hippie years of opting out, moving back to the land – and the consequent production of countless numbers of candles and strings of glass beads. The more bizarre manifestations have passed, but the theme of voluntary simplicity remains, and may well become even more significant in the future. The number of hobbyists is still increasing, as people have more leisure time at their disposal. But, as the following essay reminds us, a self-taught hobbyist like William Hazzard can develop extraordinary skills and become a professional.

Like almost all other art forms, crafts have become internationalized. The speed of communications means that anything new is transmitted round the world in a very short space of time. Unfortunately, the transmission is all two-dimensional, purely visual, and often with little idea of scale. We find a rapidly increasing number of specialized magazines, many devoted to the crafts. All of them depend heavily on colour illustrations to grab the attention of the reader, but these pictures are just as two-dimensional as the television screen and the film clip. Yet crafts are essentially *three*-dimensional and *tactile*, another quality that is almost impossible to convey in pictures. Inexperienced craftspeople try to interpret and transform these two-dimensional pictures into new three-dimensional forms with results that can sometimes be fruitful, but are too often unfortunate.

Not only are depictions of finished objects transmitted by magazines, and particularly by slide shows, but processes are disseminated as well. Thus, techniques such as *batik* or *plangi* (tie and dye) that were once restricted to particular regions are now common everywhere. Demanding techniques, like *niello* and *mokume* in metalworking, for example, are also being explored. Quilting, once thought of mainly in connection with rural quilting bees tied to traditional designs, is being used in extraordinarily imaginative ways. Only a very few craft techniques in Canada seem to be restricted to

...is one that

...roups de-

...t dates back

...ocumented

...ack to the

...was the

...e Saint-Anne

...ac there were

...in New

...ada

...e Women's

...cerned at the

...f traditional

...he craft

movement was started by women, and was run by women for many years; such men as were involved were mainly figureheads – lawyers, senators, or holders of similar respectable positions in society. The inspiration was William Morris, since many of the women retained close links with the United Kingdom. In fact, an exhibition of Canadian crafts was sent to the Home Industries and Arts Associations' show in London in 1905. In all, seventy-seven such exhibitions were dispatched between 1905 and 1910, including shows to London, Dublin and Melbourne.

In 1904, the Women's Art Association turned over their assets to what would become, in 1906, the Canadian Handicrafts Guild, later the Canadian Guild of Crafts. In 1910, a representative of the Guild travelled on a lecture tour to western Canada, and the immediate result was the establishment of Guild branches in Edmonton in 1911, Vancouver 1912, and Winnipeg 1913. In 1916, the first branch was established in the Maritimes, in Charlottetown. This guild published the first guide to home dyeing, making it available in French and English.

After taking steps to revive crafts in Quebec, the Guild became interested in Doukhobour crafts, which they bought and sold as early as 1904. They began to work with native peoples in 1907, and in the 1930s they held exhibitions of Inuit works in the McCord Museum, Montréal. In 1933 a proposed revision of the Indian Act would have prohibited Indians from wearing their traditional dress, a revision the Guild helped to defeat.

Promotion was not ignored. A brochure on Canadian crafts was produced in 1906 for distribution on steamships on the St. Lawrence, and by 1931 the government of Nova Scotia was in the business of selling crafts on Cunard boats that called at Halifax. The Guild established special prizes, including one with the help of architects in Quebec for summer cottages that used Canadian crafts in their interior design. In 1939, Ryerson Press made a film in colour of the first major crafts fair held on Sainte-Hélène Island in Montréal.

The Guild was not alone, even if it was a pioneer. Many independent associations were set up – Cape Breton Home Industries in 1927, Mount Allison Handicrafts in 1932, Charlotte County Cottage Crafts and North Lanark Weavers Guild in 1934, Victoria Island Arts and

Crafts Society in 1927, Regina Arts and Crafts Society in 1942, and so on. Little remains of many of these associations beyond a few lingering memories. Foreshadowing the provincial associations of today, provincial branches of the Guild were established in Manitoba (still going strong) and Alberta in 1928, Saskatchewan 1929, Prince Edward Island 1933, Quebec 1935 (also still in existence), and Ontario 1936.

The Depression of the thirties made great demands on all craft organizations, which provided moral and financial support to their members as well as a variety of educational programmes. The Searle Grain Company in Winnipeg undertook to train weavers; in the Maritimes the cooperative movement was well established under the sponsorship of St. Francis Xavier University; in Alberta the Guild produced radio programmes on craft techniques. Later, the Second World War, like the First, brought demands for skilled craftspeople to take part in occupational therapy programmes.

It is ironic that, even as the great surge in craft production began in the 1960s and early 1970s, the influence of the older associations was declining or was spent. It took only a few years for much of the work of the associations to be forgotten; it has taken many more years to re-establish their programmes. For example, in 1938 the Percé Handcraft Committee set up a dental clinic for its members; we have not yet re-attained that level of service, despite the establishment of many new provincial and media-based craft associations during the past fifteen

Mrs. Saidye Bronfman presenting the first Award for Excellence in the Crafts to Robin Hopper, 1977

years. These associations are determined to use new and innovative means of providing services to craftspeople.

The Saidye Bronfman Award for Excellence in the Crafts

In 1977 the Samuel and Saidye Bronfman Family Foundation decided to establish an annual award to be given over the next ten years to outstanding Canadian practitioners in the crafts. The Award was created to honour the eightieth birthday of Mrs. Saidye Bronfman, and Mrs. Bronfman herself still meets each recipient every year at her home. Peter Swann, the executive director of the Foundation at that time, whose interest in Canadian crafts goes back much farther than 1977, was invaluable in helping to bring the Award to fruition.

The Canadian Crafts Council, the successor to both the Canadian Guild of Crafts (national) and the Canadian Craftsmen's Association, was chosen to administer the Award at its inception, and has done so ever since.

A selection committee was established comprising five people: the President of the CCC, a past recipient of the Award, a director or officer of the CCC, and two others chosen at large. The selection of the recipient is made through the slides they submit, since no other method is practicable in a country as large as ours. Ideally, the Selection Committee ought to be able to see – and touch – such essentially visual and tactile objects. But this would mean incurring astronomical costs to either ship the Committee around the country or bring a range of works by the candidates to a central point, assuming that it could be done.

The criteria established for the Award state that the principle requirement is the excellence of the work – and excellence is intended to cover all aspects of aesthetics, creativity, innovation, technical mastery and so on. Secondly, the recipient must have made a substantial contribution to the development of crafts in Canada over a significant period of time. The monetary value of the Award, which is now $20,000, makes it one of the most generous and important awards granted in Canada today.

Starting in 1977, the Award was to be given for ten years, but the Bronfman Family Foundation has generously agreed to extend it for a further ten years. The results of the family's initiative and the excellence the Foundation recognized and encouraged are to be found in these pages and in the works acquired for the exhibition.

Masters of the Crafts

by Stephen Inglis and Kristin Rothschild

Until the last few decades, the crafts in Canada were adrift, not yet integrated into the arts in the minds of most Canadians. The practitioners of the handmade and the well-made often had to settle for professional marginality, but that situation has changed dramatically. Craft's historical links with architecture, design and fashion are being re-established. Among the dedicated group who have helped to restore the status of craftsmanship in Canadian society are the eleven recipients of the Saidye Bronfman Award for Excellence in the Crafts during its first decade. The masters honoured here reached a wide audience and had an important influence on a new generation of craftspeople. It is partly through their vision and that of the people whose imagination they stimulated that works of craft are now featured in public buildings, art galleries and museums.

This higher profile for the crafts coincides with a re-evaluation of the diverse streams of art production, not only in this country but all over the world. The growing acceptance of the aesthetic significance of functional objects, nurtured by greater access to non-western and ancient cultures as well as to the arts of native North Americans, has had a profound impact on the artistic tastes of Canadians. This has

become one of the most culturally diverse countries in the world. Our society not only retains elements of traditions born in other places and times, but also gives birth to new cultural patterns.

Craftspeople, as much as other creative Canadians, have acted as conduits for cultural transmission and as interpreters of the process of cultural change. Craftspeople have also contributed to reviving an awareness of the emotional and spiritual significance of handmade objects. Thus, they have begun to regain their historical role as keepers of tradition as well as innovators and harbingers of the future. They are no longer the outfitters of daily life, but rather creators of the precious objects that introduce human values in our mass-produced material culture.

Using as examples phases from the careers of the Bronfman Award recipients, this essay surveys *beginnings*, how craft skills are acquired; *choices*, how a direction becomes established; and *contributions*, how a craftsperson continues to develop and move forward. Through the experiences and choices of these masters, we sense the multiplicity of sources upon which contemporary craftspeople draw, the variety of circumstances in which they choose to work, and the ways in which they transmit their skill and

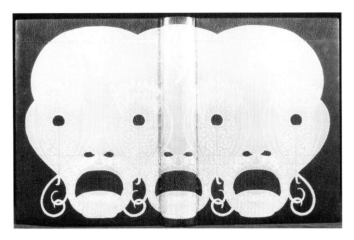

Tales of Mystery and Imagination, by Edgar Allan Poe (London, 1919), bound by Michael Wilcox in 1978 in black oasis leather with gilt-tooled fawn oasis onlays

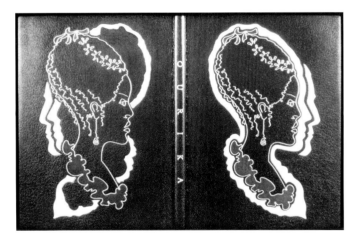

Ourika, by Claire de Durfort (Austin, Texas: W. Thomas Taylor, 1977), bound by Wilcox in 1981 in black oasis leather; Ourika's head is tooled in gilt and silhouetted against white calf

knowledge. The experiences of the Bronfman Award recipients encompass many of the challenges and opportunities facing any craftsperson in this society.

Beginnings

The experiences of Michael Wilcox, Lois Etherington Betteridge and William Hazzard identify three very different learning approaches to craft. There is the traditional course, that of the apprentice/master relationship, which teaches skills within a trade; a later adaptation of this system involves the advanced student working informally under the supervision of a master. The present-day structured approach is provided by colleges and universities, where the applied-arts student learns a variety of interdisciplinary art and craft techniques. The third route is that of the self-taught craftsperson, whose highly developed skills and single-mindedness lead to the professional arena.

Michael Wilcox

It was a combination of education and industry that Michael Wilcox sought when he apprenticed with a commercial book bindery in his hometown of Bristol, England. There, Wilcox learned that bookbinding was made up of several specialized and rigorously defined skills, each practised by a different craftsperson. He describes the system at Edward Everard, Printer:

There was this strict division of labour. Usually a binder was either a forwarder or a finisher. I did the forwarding. When I got there it was sort of at a toss of a coin whether I would be a finisher or a forwarder. They found an empty bench among the forwarders and put me there.[1]

Wilcox mastered the skill of forwarding, which involved constructing books by ruling and binding handmade papers into ledgers and sewing up the printed pages of manuscripts into books. After moving to Canada in 1962, Wilcox obtained a five-year contract restoring the University of Toronto's collection of antique medical books. This project provided him with the opportunity to refine and update his binding skills while developing related abilities in book restoration and conservation. Other private commissions encouraged him to experiment with creating original designs for book covers.

Now Wilcox is breaking new ground within the modern context of fine-design bookbinding. His craft encompasses all aspects of the trade, from binding through original cover design to the finely tooled finished product. By double-binding rare books with an inner acid-free layer covered with a leather casing, he is offering a satisfying compromise between modern conservation concerns and the traditional aesthetic values of bookbinding.

The interest that art galleries are now showing in exhibiting fine bookbinding suggests that the craft has joined other craft media in their newly attained status as art forms. Wilcox, however, does not regard himself as an artist but rather as a bookbinder and a craftsman. He insists that the craft cannot exist separately from the book and its literary content. The complicated process of bookbinding, with

Wilcox in his Woodview, Ontario, studio in 1987, holding the brass and copper block he used for stamping the main image on the *Ourika* cover

Lois Betteridge working with a student at her studio in Ottawa, 1976

its reliance on several distinct skills, also demands a keen technical mastery that takes years of practice to acquire. For these reasons, contemporary fine bookbinding may remain somewhat isolated within the craft world and removed to a degree from the other arts.

It could be his isolation and economic vulnerability that incline Wilcox to discourage aspiring young bookbinders from taking up the trade. To those who persist, however, Wilcox still recommends a good traditional apprenticeship, emphasizing technical skills of book construction, rather than condensed college or university training in modern book design. In the end, though, Wilcox feels that the chosen course of instruction really does not matter, for "Those that have got it in them to do it will do it, some way or another."

Lois Betteridge

Until about forty years ago, the apprenticeship system was virtually the only way of transmitting craft skills. Since that time, however, North American learning centres have developed a new system of skill-building. Influenced by the Bauhaus model of education, American and Canadian colleges and universities have introduced into their curricula an interdisciplinary programme of arts and crafts. Thus, fine artists, craftspeople and designers are working together to introduce students to a variety of disciplines and materials. This broader approach, de-emphasizing early vocational specialization, has helped to change the idea that craft is responsive only to its own aesthetic and to marketing considerations. Instead, the acquisition of new skills and the recovery of traditional craft techniques are encouraged within the creative university environment.

It was in this vibrant postwar learning environment that Lois Etherington Betteridge was introduced to the traditional craft of silversmithing, newly incorporated into the

Betteridge sketching a design for a new work in her Guelph, Ontario, studio in 1987

university curriculum. She says that silver-smithing

> was just starting in the States. Kansas University was the first university to teach silversmithing, and I was in my second year [there]. I didn't know silversmithing existed until I went down there. . . . I started taking it then, as a design student.

University silversmithing retained some of the techniques and attitudes of the historical silver-smith guilds, but no longer required apprentices to specialize in a distinct stage or process of silversmithing. A major reason was the influence of Scandinavian industrial design, in which the craftsperson was responsible for all technical stages. As a result, students were taught a wide range of skills. For example, Betteridge learned the value of functional design in hollow-ware (or hammer-raised silversmithing), which re-quires a technical mastery of tools and proce-dures and a knowledge of traditional materials.

She spent the next ten years refining the many technical skills required of her craft, experiment-ing with repoussé, chasing, raising and the lost-wax technique, and inlaying silver objects with ebony, horn and precious stones. Public and private commissions challenged Betteridge to produce secular hollow-ware and ecclesiastical silver, which she viewed as "the ultimate compromise of making the functional object sculptural, but not sculpture."

Even in this most traditional of crafts, new issues continually emerge. The relevance of non-functional hollow-ware in contemporary silver-smithing, for example, is a topic that Betteridge debates with peers and a new generation of silversmiths. The application of high technology in craft manufacture and the use of synthetic materials, such as space-age ceramics and plas-tics, are also provoking animated discussion. Betteridge views these developments with some concern, fearing that traditional skills and craftsmanship will be quickly replaced by the shortcut approach: "Don't solder it, bolt it."

In support of her beliefs, Lois Betteridge has assumed a high profile within the international metalsmithing community, teaching traditional silversmithing skills to apprentices in her studio, giving lectures to students, and participating in professional panel discussions and workshops with her peers. Her recognized professional status demonstrates to aspiring silversmiths that it is possible to make a career of traditional silversmithing today.

William Hazzard

Self-taught wood carving may seem a world away from the guild craft of metalsmithing. But perfection of skills is also the goal of Saskatche-wan wildlife carver William Hazzard, whose self-taught origins typify a third means of acquiring craft skills in Canada. Hazzard's introduction into the craft world was fortuitous; his success, though, has been remarkable.

As a young man, Hazzard enjoyed sketching the wildlife of rural Saskatchewan, where he grew up, and he took pride in the fact that his drawings were good likenesses of his subjects. Many years later, during a long and confining convalescence in 1972–73, Hazzard looked for useful work to occupy his hands.

I was looking for something in the arts. I didn't know if it was going to be carving or painting. . . . My wife said, "Why don't you go down and do some carving, or something; you like working with wood." So that's when I started studying birds and started carving.

He carved his first wooden bird in his basement workshop from a reproduction of a poorly painted picture of a hawk. Later, he began to sketch birds in the field, study stuffed mounts and birdskins, and emulate the wildlife carvings of Bernie Smith, a talented local craftsman. With less than four years of carving experience, he was coaxed into submitting some of his own work to the international carving

William Hazzard (left foreground) judging entries at the World Championship Wildfowl Carving Competition, Ocean City, Maryland, in 1987

Bernie Smith, a wildlife carver of Mossbank, Saskatchewan, 1986, whose work first inspired William Hazzard to perfect his own carving skills

competition in Maryland. Hazzard left with fifteen ribbons in the novice class of wildlife carving. Since those early days, he has been awarded a roomful of trophies and plaques, and his carvings have travelled the globe as part of a prestigious world tour of nature art.

Public interest in Hazzard's wildlife carvings appears to be part of a much larger contemporary fascination with accurate depictions of wildlife. This fascination may in turn derive from a universal nostalgia for the rapidly diminishing wilderness, new public awareness of ecological issues, and the immediate appeal of wildlife art. In spite of its popularity, and perhaps in part because of it, wildlife art has

The Cliche family, Saint-Joseph-de-Beauce, Quebec, ca. 1900

little status in conventional fine-art circles, where it is sometimes viewed as illustrative or representational and lacking in interpretive or spiritual dimensions.

It is true that the interpretive freedom of the wildlife carver can be inhibited by the rigid rules imposed by competitions, which can include three classes of carvers, up to seven judging categories, and as many as three thousand entrants. And there can be little discussion of carving and painting techniques with other carvers, owing to the fierce competition for recognition. Despite these constraints, international carving competitions have motivated hobbyists such as Hazzard to develop their own style and to experiment with new techniques to more skilfully depict wildlife in wood. It is this challenge to make "a better bird" that sustains William Hazzard's creative vitality.

Choices

Having achieved a basic repertoire of skills, craftspeople have to follow their own creative direction, identifying goals and seeking artistic maturity. This process takes time and the choices are varied. Some craftspeople, as for example Monique Cliche-Spénard, look to their ancestry and regional roots. Others immerse themselves in the cultural traditions of other societies as well as their own, as did Micheline Beauchemin. The potter, Wayne Ngan, made yet another choice. Drawing on both ancient and modern sources, he seeks integration with the environment in terms of both his personal life and his craft.

Monique Cliche-Spénard

A native of the Chaudière River valley in Quebec's Beauce region, Monique Cliche-Spénard is a direct descendant of one of the region's eighteenth-century seigneurial families. Acting on her father's conviction that "a people without tradition is a dying people"[2] and on her own belief that "all will be lost when our families no longer remember those things", she sought to depict the old ways of her people, the Beaucerons.

Cliche-Spénard's interest in woven fabrics led her to collect a variety of antique Beauce textiles, as well as hand-carved butter and sugar moulds, to preserve them from neglect and commercial exploitation. She researched and documented the quilts in her antique textile collection, studied traditional quilting techniques from the women of the Beauce, and began to construct

The convent and orphanage at Saint-Joseph-de-Beauce, from a postcard, ca. 1900

Quilting at the Atelier Monique Cliche-Spénard, Saint-Joseph-de-Beauce, 1979; the artist is second from left

her own unique quilts. The first quilt she made depicted traditional sugar moulds.

I wanted to tell people about the Beauce and I was looking for a visual means of doing it. Having a collection of sugar moulds at home, I thought of enlarging the patterns and explaining to people the reasons for sugar moulds at that time. I made a quilt. That was when I became known.[3]

In the course of instructing others in the craft of quilting, Cliche-Spénard came to distinguish between *l'art traditionnel*, which highlights folk-art motifs and traditional techniques of Beauce quilting, and *l'art populaire*, which emphasizes contemporary graphic design and the quilter's personal statement. A modern-day daughter of the Beauce, Cliche-Spénard applied these distinctions to her own work, reinterpreting the memories of a collective past, reassembling traditional motifs, adapting old techniques, and selecting printed and coloured fabrics for their design and effect.

Cliche-Spénard also insisted upon the economic viability of quilting. Wishing to encourage more Quebec women to profit from one of their traditional crafts, she began to involve neighbours in the production of quilts as a cottage industry. She now has an atelier where Beauce women, trained in all aspects of the business, produce and market quilts of Cliche-Spénard's design.

The success of the atelier has freed Cliche-Spénard to design and work on her own limited-edition quilts. At times she finds her art-school training and artistic ambitions at odds

Micheline Beauchemin with some of her early tapestries on the occasion of her first solo exhibition, Galerie Denyse Delrue, Montréal, 1959

with the conservative views of some of her neighbours. Nevertheless, these differences fuel a creative tension in her craft, and traditional Beauce quilting is transformed from bedcover to wall-hanging, and from utilitarian object to an artistic and political statement about the folk traditions of the Beauce and its people.

Micheline Beauchemin

For Micheline Beauchemin, the process of artistic development has always been free-spirited and continuous. Her passionate pursuit of creative expression has generated self-directed study and the mastery of several crafts in many different parts of the world.

Speaking of her early training at the École des beaux-arts de Montréal, she praises the creative and open-minded instruction of Alfred Pellan and Jean Benoit. In Paris, she studied drawing and stained-glass making, and at Mistras, Greece, renewed her convent-school skills in embroidery. At Chartres, France, Beauchemin hooked her first rugs and tapestries.

Returning to Montréal, she worked as a costume designer for stage and television, and became interested in the creation of theatre curtains. Unfortunately, neither the technology nor the opportunity to do such large-scale

Beauchemin working with assistants on the Opera curtain for the National Arts Centre, Ottawa, in Kyoto, Japan, 1968

weaving was available to her at that time in Canada. Undeterred, Beauchemin travelled to Japan, where artisans working on the wall restoration of the Imperial Palace introduced her to the craft of large-scale weaving and to Japanese fibres.

On the basis of woven samples prepared during this visit and subsequent trips to Japan, Beauchemin won contracts to design and construct two massive theatre curtains, one for the Opera of the National Arts Centre in Ottawa and the other for the Place des Arts in Montréal.

The success of these major undertakings confirmed Beauchemin's artistic future as a weaver, and enabled her to continue pushing back the boundaries of traditional weaving. Beauchemin has taken weaving off the loom, expanding its volume, length and breadth. Traditional high-warp and low-warp woven tapestries have evolved into double-sided mobiles and synthetic-fibre walls. Her repertoire of materials has grown to include unique combinations of handspun wool, silk and other natural fibres, as well as nylon, aluminum, and gold and silver threads.

Beauchemin's continuing interest in fibre arts has inspired her to study weaving techniques in Mexico, Cambodia, India and South America. For her, the technical sophistication and timeless quality of prehistoric textiles is a challenge for modern weavers. Speaking of a pre-Columbian textile, she said:

To see, to know that was done such a long time ago, by hand, and by people who had the same

Beauchemin installing one of her large architectural commissions, *The Golden Birds*, in the city hall of North York, Ontario, 1977

preoccupation as I have, as we have! . . . You look at the textile, and you know that the question was asked three thousand years ago, the same as you ask today, and the answer: There is no change.

Beauchemin nourishes this creative flow by maintaining a home base in a restored seventeenth-century farmhouse at Grondines, on the north shore of the St. Lawrence River. Situated near the village of Cap-Santé, where she vacationed in her youth, the house provides a link between her own past and her French-Canadian heritage. Within this familiar and tranquil environment, Beauchemin constructs massive tapestries and fibre sculptures for installation in public buildings all over the world. She has transported the ancient skills of weaving into the modern world of fibre art.

Wayne Ngan

The artistic talents of Wayne Ngan were evident to his Canadian teachers shortly after he arrived in Vancouver from his native China at the age of thirteen, and he was encouraged to go on to the Vancouver School of Art. Although Ngan was especially interested in painting, he could not afford the necessary materials and was obliged to enrol in the least expensive studio course, pottery. Graduating with honours, Ngan set up his own pottery and sculpture studio, began to teach, and gave pottery workshops. Later, he settled on Hornby Island, off the west coast of British Columbia. This move signalled a turning point in Ngan's development as a craftsman, since it established his dedicated commitment to ceramics and initiated the process of integrating his craft with his environment.

For four years, Ngan lived in a temporary shelter while building a kiln and continuing to make pots. From the stone and driftwood he collected around the island, he eventually created a house, a studio and a kiln shed. Within this stimulating island environment, Ngan renewed his interest in his Oriental heritage, and began experimenting with raku pottery, salt glazes and Chinese brush techniques.

Later he travelled to China to study traditional pottery styles and techniques and to Japan to work with a master potter. Preferring the spontaneity and directness of ancient Oriental pottery, Ngan was particularly impressed by the pure forms and etched decorative surfaces of China's Song dynasty and Korea's Yi dynasty. On his return to Hornby Island, he began to adapt these pottery styles and techniques to his own ceramic vessels.

Now Ngan often uses a kick wheel instead of the electric wheel, preferring the physical communication between the clay and the potter's hands and feet. He often fires green pottery in a wood-fired, instead of an electrically heated, kiln to produce a soft-hued ceramic glaze. Working in this way, Ngan not only participates directly, that is physically and spiritually, in the firing of his pottery, but also carries on an ancient Oriental tradition. It is in these ways that he contributes to a wider appreciation of Asian aesthetics in Canada, especially on the West

Wayne Ngan in Japan, during a working visit with master potter Yoichi Murakami in 1978

Coast, where the Oriental influence is prominent in architecture, landscaping and the visual arts.

Ngan's integration of craft and environment is a continuous process. He intends to further explore local materials, using Hornby Island stone in making glazes and British Columbia clay for his stoneware. He also has aspirations to become better recognized as a painter and sculptor. For the present, though, his contemplation of two interwoven heritages and the integration of local materials into his craft, home and studio have brought a certain elemental harmony into his life. Reflecting on one of his pots, Ngan recognizes that

> *it's almost like a Song dynasty pot, but somehow it's not the same because I digest those Song pots and ancient pottery and recreate my own liveliness. You can't just copy something from the past – you have to live your own life, living with your forms, and then they become part of you.*

Ngan firing his reconstruction of a Song-dynasty kiln, Hornby Island, British Columbia, in 1988

Contributions

All the Bronfman Award recipients are well established; yet they strive to create larger and more knowledgeable audiences for their own work and for that of other craftspeople. Robin Hopper has dedicated much of his career to teaching, giving workshops, and writing books on the history and technology of pottery making. Textile artist Joanna Staniszkis combines teaching with commissioned works, many of them for public buildings. Dedicated to the evolution and refinement of their pottery, Doucet–Saito are seeking a wider audience through the creation of murals and of ceramics that can be reproduced in stone and metal for a variety of public installations. Bill Reid's studio has provided on-the-job training to a succession of carvers and jewellers, and has been the focus for major sculptural projects that have provoked new respect for fine craftsmanship.

Robin Hopper

Robin Hopper feels that he acquired little technical knowledge of ceramics at art college in England, where he grew up. However, he did gain a rich historical appreciation of European, classical, and Oriental aesthetics. Beyond this formal training, Hopper was influenced by three prominent British potters. William Staite Murray and Hans Coper were among the first British potters of this century to use modern studio pottery as a personal medium of expression. Bernard Leach, who was born in China, brought the styles and techniques of Oriental functional pottery to the Western world.

Robin Hopper in his first studio, Kintbury Pottery, Berkshire, England, 1965

clays over rigid forms to reflect the eighteenth-century Japanese technique of *neriage*. He altered the chemistry of ceramic glazes and colours, and applied multiple glazes onto wheel-thrown pottery. Later, he was drawn to the ceramic accomplishments of ancient Mediterranean cultures.

Passing on the results of this research to his students, apprentices and interested professionals, Hopper has demonstrated tremendous skill and energy as communicator. As a teacher, he emphasizes the technical aspects of ceramics to his students rather than its aesthetics, which he feels can be developed independently of scientific knowledge.

In his books, Hopper passes on what he has learned about ceramic glazes and colour, pottery forms, and the history of ceramics. He has juried numerous exhibitions, and has conducted

These were the influences Hopper brought to bear in his teaching and in his studio after emigrating to Canada in 1968. Hopper experimented with the medium, seeking a more scientific understanding of his craft and rediscovering ancient techniques of pottery manufacture. He manipulated different-coloured clays to recreate the seventh-century Chinese method of making agateware, and moulded contrasting

Hopper firing at his first Canadian pottery studio, Hillsdale, Ontario, in 1975

Hopper working on the wheel at 'Chosin Pottery, a studio he set up at Metchosin, near Victoria, in 1980

workshops and given lectures at symposia in Canada, the United States, Japan, New Zealand and Great Britain. He has also served as a director, founding member or board representative on several craft councils, and continues teaching at the Metchosin International Summer School of the Arts, which he co-founded in 1985.

Participating in all these activities has its drawbacks, however, as Hopper is obliged to schedule time for the production of his own work within a full agenda of tours and lectures. Yet Hopper appears to thrive on this hectic pace, and his technical mastery, ability to demystify the chemistry of ceramics, and willingness over many years to share the results of his research have already influenced a generation of potters. His dedicated enthusiasm and participation in a contemporary ceramic tradition continues to influence the ways in which potters produce both functional ware and one-of-a-kind exhibition pieces.

Joanna Staniszkis

Teaching has also been the vehicle Joanna Staniszkis chose for communicating her extensive knowledge of weaving and tapestry making to others. As a young art student in Warsaw, Poland, and later at the Art Institute of Chicago, Staniszkis worked towards a career in interior design. Her plans had to be revised, however, after she was introduced to the loom and "discovered the magic of putting threads across and coming up with a piece of fabric." Not long after she graduated from the Art Institute of

Joanna Staniszkis (centre), her long-time associate Anthoula Stavridis (far left), and project assistants on the scaffolding erected to execute a large tapestry commission, *Treasures*, for the Grosvenor International Building, Vancouver, in 1985

Chicago, Staniszkis was able to combine her talents in weaving and interior design in a teaching position at the University of British Columbia. There she has developed a tapestry and weaving programme that incorporates inter-disciplinary course work with the university's School of Architecture and Museum of Anthropology.

Staniszkis's own studio work has evolved alongside her career as a professor, and has influenced the formation of her students. Over the years, their work has reflected her early professional interest in texture and her preference for handspun yarns and natural dyes as well as her later experiments in form and construction methods. This close association of her own professional development with that of her students illustrates, for Staniszkis, both the difficulty of keeping her two worlds of teaching and studio work separate and the need to do so. Still, she recognizes the advantages that her studio work affords her students, acquainting them, through her own experiences, with the world of the professional artist.

Her concern for her profession extends to the construction of tapestries. Durability is a concern, as works displayed in public spaces are exposed to environmental stress from excessive heat and cold, light and dust. To this end, Staniszkis has researched antique and contemporary art-forms of other cultures for durable materials and different techniques. Staniszkis feels that she fulfils a personal responsibility to her craft by assuring the longevity of her work in terms of both sensitive design and durable materials. This ensures a continuous climate of support and goodwill between the public, the patron and the textile artist.

Doucet–Saito

A fusion of sensibilities – personal, cultural and aesthetic – in both life and work has been the objective of the ceramic artists known professionally as Doucet–Saito. When they first met, in a pottery workshop in North Hatley, Quebec, Louise Doucet was a graduate of the School of Art and Design, Montreal Museum of Fine Arts, and Satoshi Saito was a Tokyo-born graduate student studying economics at McGill University. Sharing a common interest in ceramics, they married and went to Japan to study with pottery masters. Since their return to Canada, they have worked together on a farm in the Eastern Townships of Quebec.

For Doucet–Saito, life in Canada has liberated them from following any particular ceramic tradition, leaving them free to draw inspiration from the great works of Oriental ceramic art as well as from ancient Pre-Columbian, Greek, Egyptian and Etruscan art. Through their dedicated efforts to perfect their skills, research

Hommage to Mies van der Rohe (detail), a Staniszkis tapestry installed at the Toronto-Dominion Centre, Toronto, in 1985

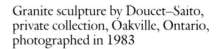

Satoshi and Louise Saito firing a
wood-burning kiln at Mashiko,
Japan, April 1967

Granite sculpture by Doucet–Saito,
private collection, Oakville, Ontario,
photographed in 1983

local clays, and explore the formal qualities of
the ceramic medium, Doucet–Saito have
achieved a sophisticated mastery of their craft.
Gradually, their vessels have evolved into expressions of pure form.

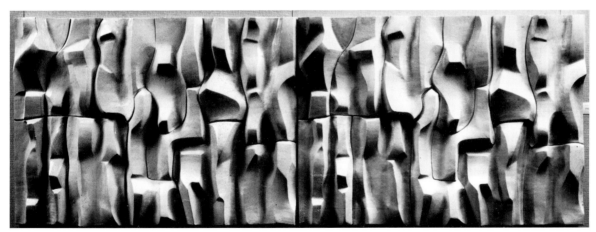

Ceramic mural by Doucet–Saito,
Imperial Life Assurance Company of
Canada, Toronto, photographed in
1985

That some critics classify their work as ceramics and others as sculpture is irrelevant to Doucet–Saito. Their interest lies in creating, together, ceramic works that communicate directly to the viewer something of the joy, risk and reward that is their life and art.

Bill Reid

Bill Reid, one of Canada's foremost metalsmiths, has played an important part in the movement to call attention to the great artistic achievements of Canada's native peoples. Born of Haida-Indian and Scottish-American parentage, Reid did not know that he was "anything other than an average Caucasian North American" until he was in his early teens.[4] In 1943, in an effort to discover the traditions of his maternal ancestors, Reid made the first of what have become annual pilgrimages to the Haida village of Skidegate in the Queen Charlotte Islands. There he visited with his grandfather, Charles Gladstone, a top-notch boat builder who had been an apprentice of Charles Edenshaw, the great nineteenth-century Haida carver and silversmith. Reid's grandfather, who was Edenshaw's nephew, stood last in a direct line of Haida makers of silver jewellery. Fascinated by Haida design, Reid began exploring its structure through training and experimentation in European-style jewellery making. He gradually moved away from his career as a CBC broadcaster toward that of artist. He has designed and made gold and silver jewellery, done wood carving, designed silk-screen prints, and written and illustrated books.

In striving to understand and share the structure and meaning of Haida art, Reid has passed along his passion and his knowledge to a new generation of Northwest Coast artists. While most of their production is destined for the marketplace, an increasing number of works are being created for the native community for ceremonial use and as potlatch gifts.

While Reid admits to playing a part in the regeneration of aspects of native heritage, he is as aware as anyone that a true cultural revival

Bill Reid sawing a block of argillite, Queen Charlotte Islands, late 1950s

involves a commitment to land rights and to political and social development. His own opposition to the logging of the Queen Charlottes and his attempts to involve Haida communities in projects like canoe building express his commitment.

The work of Bill Reid, and that of younger artists who have been inspired by his example, has become the focus of positive new discussions between native and non-native communities. As a museum curator and writer, Reid has helped to reveal the artistic achievements of the Haida. In his large-scale projects, he has set in motion the collaboration of skilled carvers and other craftspeople from a variety of traditions.

Reid's commitment to craftsmanship evidently goes beyond any particular culture or ethnic group. He points to the crucial role of the maker in "a world where we more and more seek out and admire the finely crafted object, [but] we less and less know how to make it."[5] Reid speaks with the faith of all great craftspeople when he asserts:

> *Once we discard our ethnocentric hierarchical ideas about the way the world works, we will find that one basic quality unites all the works of mankind that speak to us in human, recognizable voices across the barriers of time, culture and space: the simple quality of being well made.*[6]

This survey of the recipients of the Saidye Bronfman Award has revealed ten different experiences and approaches in lives devoted to craftsmanship. Yet, a consideration of their individual careers also goes a long way towards

Reid carving a Haida pole, Skidegate, Queen Charlotte Islands, 1977

tracing the primary directions of the modern craft movement in Canada. Through their work we sense the strength of regional attachments, the complex interaction of various cultural traditions, and the interplay between Canada's cities and its vast hinterland.

All are now acknowledged as masters of their craft. There is, of course, a danger in being a senior member of any creative community, in that some of one's earlier designs or techniques are bound to have suffered from overexposure or become outdated by the time that recognition is received. The fact that these eleven masters are sometimes subject to criticism by younger, less conventional artists, not to mention critics, is a natural response to a vigorous cultural movement.

The Bronfman Award is now well into its second decade and more masters are being named. Already selected are Carol Sabiston, textile artist of Victoria, and Lutz Haufschild, glass artist of Toronto.

It is part of a rite of passage, a maturing of the Canadian crafts movement as a whole, that we begin to acknowledge the heroes of our own country and era. Some are included in these pages. Others will join them each year. This can hardly remove them from the ongoing debates and evolving issues that are integral to being a creative person in Canada. All are continuing their work and the collective discovery it implies.

Notes

1 Unless otherwise indicated, the quoted passages throughout the text are transcriptions from taped interviews conducted by Stephen Inglis with the Bronfman Award recipients in 1985 and 1986. The tapes are in the collection of the Museum's Canadian Centre for Folk Culture Studies (ING-Ac-8 to 17).
2 Richard Hotte, "Un nouveau mode d'expression dans l'art de la courtepointe au Québec". Master's thesis, Université Laval, 1985.
3 Transcribed from a taped interview conducted with Monique Cliche-Spénard by Nicole Grenier on 18 June 1986. Collection of the Canadian Centre for Folk Culture Studies (GRE-Ac-1, 2).
4 Bill Reid, "Curriculum Vitae", in *Bill Reid: A Retrospective Exhibition* (Vancouver: Vancouver Art Gallery, 1974), not paginated.
5 Bill Reid, Introduction to *Bill Koochin* (Burnaby, B.C.: Burnaby Art Gallery, 1980), 2.
6 Ibid.

Select Bibliography

Books and Exhibition Catalogues

Abrahamson, Una. *Crafts Canada: The Useful Arts.* Toronto: Clarke Irwin, 1974.

Boulizon, Guy. *L'artisanat créateur au Québec.* Montréal: Hurtubise HMH, 1985.

Bovey, Patricia E. *Robin Hopper: Ceramic Explorations, 1957–1987.* North York, Ont.: Koffler Gallery and the Art Gallery of Greater Victoria, 1987.

Burnaby Art Gallery. *Bill Koochin.* Burnaby, B.C., 1980.

Burnham, Dorothy K. *The Comfortable Arts: Traditional Spinning and Weaving in Canada.* Ottawa: National Gallery of Canada, 1981.

Canadian Crafts Council. *Artisan '78: The First National Travelling Exhibition of Contemporary Canadian Crafts.* Ottawa, 1979.

————. Atlantic Caucus. *Atlantic Visions: Crafts from Canada's Four Atlantic Provinces.* Charlottetown, [1982].

Canadian Jewellers Association. *Jewellery Today: A Source Book for the Industry.* Toronto, n.d.

Duffek, Karen. *Bill Reid: Beyond the Essential Form.* Museum Note, no. 19. Vancouver: University of British Columbia Press, 1986.

Galerie d'art du parc. *3ᵉ Biennale nationale de céramique, du 24 juin au 28 août 1988.* Trois-Rivières, Que., 1988.

Grand Prix des métiers d'art. *Grand Prix des métiers d'art, 1987, New York–Montréal.* Montréal, 1987.

Green, H. Gordon. *A Heritage of Canadian Handicrafts.* Toronto: McClelland & Stewart, 1967.

Hogbin, Stephen. *Wood Turning: The Purpose of the Object.* Toronto: Van Nostrand Reinhold, 1980.

Hopper, Robin. *The Ceramic Spectrum: A Simplified Approach to Glaze and Color Development.* Radnor, Penn.: Chilton Book Company, 1984.

————. *Explorations within a Landscape: New Porcelain by Robin Hopper.* Victoria: Published by the author, 1978.

————. *Functional Pottery: Form and Aesthetic in Pots of Purpose.* Radnor, Penn.: Chilton Book Company, 1986.

Inglis, Stephen. *Contemporary Craft: The Human Touch.* Oracle, no. 58. Ottawa: National Museum of Man, 1985.

Jones, D.G. *Doucet–Saito: Concepts in Clay.* North York, Ont.: Koffler Gallery, 1985.

Leigh Yawkey Woodson Art Museum. *The 1984 Birds in Art Exhibition.* Wisconsin, 1984.

Lucie-Smith, Edward. *The Story of Craft: The Craftsman's Role in Society.* Ithaca, N.Y.: Cornell University Press, 1981.

Massey Foundation. *The Craftsman's Way: Canadian Expressions.* Toronto: University of Toronto Press, 1981.

Metropolitan Museum of Art. *Bindings by Michael Wilcox.* New York, 1983.

National Gallery of Canada. *Canadian Fine Crafts, 1966/67.* Ottawa: Queen's Printer, 1966.

National Museum of Man. *Works of Craft from the Massey Foundation Collection.* Balmuir Book Publishing in cooperation with the National Museums of Canada, 1984.

National Museum of Natural Sciences. *Lois Betteridge, Silversmith*. Ottawa, [1981].

Needleman, Carla. *The Work of Craft: An Inquiry into the Nature of Crafts and Craftsmanship*. New York: Knopf, 1979; Avon, 1981.

Olympic Arts Festival. *Restless Legacies: Contemporary Craft Practice in Canada*. Calgary: XV Olympic Winter Games Organizing Committee, 1988.

Paz, Octavio, and the World Crafts Council. *In Praise of Hands: Contemporary Crafts of the World*. Toronto: McClelland & Stewart, 1974.

Reid, Bill. *Bill Reid: A Retrospective Exhibition*. Vancouver: Vancouver Art Gallery, 1974.

Russ, Joel, and Lynn, Lou. *Contemporary Stained Glass: A Portfolio of Canadian Work*. Toronto: Doubleday, 1985.

Shadbolt, Doris. *Bill Reid*. Vancouver and Toronto: Douglas & McIntyre, 1986.

Simard, Cyril. *Artisanat québécois*. 4 vols. Montréal: Éditions de l'Homme, 1975–77.

Smith, Philip. *The Book: Art and Object*. Merstham, England: Published by the author, 1982.

Thompson, R.J. *Down to Earth: Canadian Potters at Work*. Toronto: Nelson, 1980.

Wilcox, Michael. *Twelve Bindings: Michael Wilcox*. Austin, Texas: W. Thomas Taylor, 1985.

Williams, Gerry, ed. *Apprenticeship in Craft*. New Hampshire: Daniel Clark Books, 1981.

Yanagi, Soetsu. *The Unknown Craftsman: A Japanese Insight into Beauty*. Tokyo: Kodansha International, 1972.

Articles

Allison, Glenn. "Pottery by Wayne Ngan". *Canada Crafts*, March 1979: 22–25.

Amyot, Lucie. "Doucet–Saito". *Fusion* 10, no. 2 (Winter 1987): 17–19.

Barros, Anne. "The Metal Arts Guild of Ontario". *Metalsmith*, Spring 1984: 43–44.

Betteridge, Lois Etherington. "The Smith's Mandate: Looking at the Future". *Metalsmith*, Fall 1986: 8–11.

Bland, Mavis. "Robin Hopper". *Ceramics Monthly*, April 1973: 35.

De Santana, Hubert. "Wildlife at the Top". *Canadian Art*, Spring 1986: 58–65.

Downey, Roger. "Apprentice to a Lost Art [Bill Reid]". *Pacific Northwest*, October 1983: 36–40.

Hotte, Richard. "Un nouveau mode d'expression dans l'art de la courtepointe au Québec [Monique Cliche-Spénard]". Master's thesis. Université Laval, 1985.

Hryniuk, Margaret. "Wildfowl Sculptor [William Hazzard]". *Canadian Collector*, January/February 1985: 43–45.

Iglauer, Edith. "The Myth Maker [Bill Reid]". *Saturday Night*, February 1982: 13–24.

Inglis, Stephen. "The Island of Craft . . . and an Outgoing Tide". *Museum* (Unesco), no. 157 (1988): 34–38.

Jones, D.G. "Doucet–Saito: Momentum in Clay". *artscanada*, August/September 1979: 36–37.

———. "Louise and Satoshi Doucet-Saito". *Ceramics Monthly*, April 1982: 28–31.

Kawgas, Matthew. "Robin Hopper". *Ceramics Monthly*, August 1988: 48.

Larue-Langlois, Jacques. "Doucet–Saito: La poterie du geste a une âme". *Forces* 49 (4th quarter 1979): 30–32.

"Lois Betteridge – Winner of Bronfman Award 1978". *Craftsman* 3, no. 6 (December 1978): cover, 2–3.

Lowndes, Joan. "Child of the Raven, Bill Reid". *Vanguard*, February 1982: 20–25.

Lucie-Smith, Edward. "Craft Today: Historical Roots and Contemporary Perspectives". In *American Craft Today: Poetry of the Physical*, by Paul J. Smith, 15–40. New York: American Craft Council and Weidenfeld & Nicolson, 1983.

Lush, Pat. "A Transformer of Existing Things [Bill Reid]". *Ryerson Rambler* 28 (Fall 1985): 9–13.

Mulaire, Bernard. "20th Century Bookbinding". *Ontario Craft*, Spring 1983: 19–23.

"1981 Bronfman Winner [Joanna K. Staniszkis]". *Artisan*, Fall 1981: 8.

"1982 Bronfman Award Winner [Micheline Beauchemin]". *Artisan*, Summer 1982: 12–13.

"Quebec Quiltmaker [Monique Cliche-Spénard] Wins Bronfman Award". *Artisan News*, May–June 1979: 9.

Racette, Gilles. "Louise Doucet: La terre comme rythme". *Vie des Arts* 18, no. 74 (Spring 1974): 14–17; English transl., "The Rhythm of the Earth", 92.

Reeves, John. "The Right Space . . . Micheline Beauchemin". *Canadian Art*, Fall 1984: 60–61.

Reid, Bill. "'The Legacy' Review Reviewed". *Vanguard*, October/November 1982: 34–35.

Robert, Guy. "Micheline Beauchemin – Des signes qui s'amplifient". *Vie des Arts* 25, no. 102 (Spring 1981): 20–24.

"Robin Hopper Wins First Bronfman Award". *Artisan News*, November–December 1977: 9.

Ross, Judy. "At Home with Robin Hopper". *Western Living*, December 1986: 30–32e.

Saito, Satoshi. "La céramique, une façon de vivre". *Critère* 12 (May 1975): 21–28.

Shadbolt, Doris. "The Transparency of Clay". *Fusion* 10, no. 2 (Winter 1987): 5–8.

Smith, Adam. "Michael Wilcox, Bookbinder". *Ontario Craft*, Spring 1985: 12–15.

"The Very Best in Bird Art". *Orange Disk*, Summer 1982: 8–13.

Viau, René. "Micheline Beauchemin: Tapisserie et environnement/ Tapestry and Environment". *Architecture Contemporaine/Contemporary Architecture* (Lausanne, Switzerland), vol. 4 (1982–83): 20–24, 119–23.

"Wayne Ngan, 7th Bronfman Recipient". *Artisan*, Summer 1983: 2–4.

Wyman, Max. "New Dawn at Skidegate: Bill Reid and the Haida". *Beaver*, June/July 1986: 48–56.

Sound Recordings

Grenier, Nicole. Interview with Monique Cliche-Spénard, 18 June 1986. Collection of the Canadian Centre for Folk Culture Studies, Canadian Museum of Civilization. GRE-Ac-1, 2.

Inglis, Stephen. Interviews with Bronfman Award recipients. Collection of the Canadian Centre for Folk Culture Studies, Canadian Museum of Civilization.

- Beauchemin, Micheline. 5 June 1986. ING-Ac-13, 14.
- Betteridge, Lois Etherington. 23 August 1985 and 22 March 1986. ING-Ac-10, 11.
- Hazzard, William. 6 August 1985 and 15 March 1986. ING-Ac-8, 9, 12.
- Hopper, Robin. 10 August 1985. ING-Ac-9.
- Ngan, Wayne. 12 August 1985 and 22 May 1986. ING-Ac-9, 16.
- Staniszkis, Joanna. 26 May 1986. ING-Ac-16, 17.
- Wilcox, Michael. 16 July 1986. ING-Ac-15.

The Artists and Their Works

In this section the artists appear in the order in
which they received the annual Saidye Bronfman
Award for Excellence in the Crafts.

Among the works shown, the majority are from
the collection of the Canadian Centre for Folk
Culture Studies, Canadian Museum of Civilization. These are identified by their accession
number, preceded by the initials *CMC*. Where the
works were acquired through the generosity of
the Samuel and Saidye Bronfman Family Foundation, the word *Bronfman* follows the accession
number. Other donors and lenders are also
gratefully acknowledged in the captions to the
illustrations.

Dimensions are given from the largest to the
smallest measure, and are in centimetres.

'Chosin Pottery, the studio and home of ceramist Robin Hopper and his wife, Judi Dyelle, is an oasis. Entering the circular driveway, one is immediately impressed with the artist's diversity of interests and his accomplishments. The gardens are carefully planned, with fruit trees, flowing water, fish, rhododendrons, bonsai, fig trees, and expanses of green. Their house is ahead and the studio is under the trees, off to the left. The showroom, attached to the house, faces the studio. The air is one of tranquillity, but on entering the house, studio or showroom one quickly realizes that 'Chosin Pottery is always full of creative energy.

Work is in progress in the studio, with pieces in every stage of creation. Visitors come and go to the showroom. Prospective students telephone, either asking to work with the artist himself or seeking a place in the Metchosin International Summer School of the Arts. Calls come too from Robin's publisher regarding his third book, now under way. Colleagues, associations, galleries and art schools frequently invite him to lecture, lend pieces to an exhibition, or even coordinate a solo or group show. Despite these tangential activities over the past thirty years, and particularly since receiving the first Saidye Bronfman Award for Excellence in the Crafts, in 1977, Robin Hopper has been prolific in his production of ceramics – both functional wares and one-of-a-kind pieces – and uncompromising in the high standards he sets for himself.

Robin Hopper, the teacher, author and ceramic artist of international acclaim, is above all a knowledgeable, lively, generous individual. Our first meeting, some seven years ago, took place at his Metchosin home and studio near Victoria, British Columbia, where he had invited me to discuss the historical and contemporary issues of the fine art of ceramics. This "Renaissance man" led our discourse through not only art history but also economic history, the social and cultural past, literature, music, and of course physics and chemistry, the scientific base of ceramics. His knowledge is as deep as it is vast, learned through looking, reading and handling. His vivid visual memory allows him almost instant recall of the whereabouts of any piece – his own or those historical works which over the years have challenged him in terms of colour or glaze, form or balance, history or source. These are the pieces he has reproduced in his books, *The Ceramic Spectrum* and *Functional Pottery*, and it is these that provide the historical context for his lectures on ceramics and the ceramic spectrum.

Through Robin's work one sees his consistent interest in civilizations past and cultures present. The many ideas derived from his travels, his curiosity, his scientific understanding, and his ongoing experimentation and exploration have resulted in unique colours and glazes and in interesting combinations of form and design. But one example is his Feather Basket Series, combining forms of the native peoples of the Northwest Coast, the reflection of trees in the water at nearby Witty's Lagoon, Robin's interest in geological land formations, and his enjoyment of blue and white.

Hopper's relationship to the land combines the approach of the painter and the ceramist. He recorded his observations of clouds, land, colours and atmospheric impressions (all detailed in terms of glaze recipes) in a notebook while driving across Canada in 1977, when he moved his studio and family from Ontario to Vancouver Island. These notes formed both the basis of his Landscape Series of 1977 and 1978 and the theme of his exhibition "Explorations within a Landscape" following his receipt of the Bronfman Award. The gardener in him and his interest in atmospheric colour effects have recently resurfaced in his Hibiscus and Clematis series. Both plants bloom in his own garden.

Everyone who visits Robin's showroom or hears him lecture is immediately impressed with his openness. He is always ready to share techniques, glaze recipes, thought processes and ideas. A rich aesthetic and intellectual experience awaits any visitor or student!

Patricia E. Bovey
Director
Art Gallery of Greater Victoria
Victoria

Landscape Plate 1979
Porcelain, hand-built
Multiple glazes, trailed, poured and brushed; glaze intaglio through wax resist
36 × 36 × 10
CMC 86-116 (Bronfman)

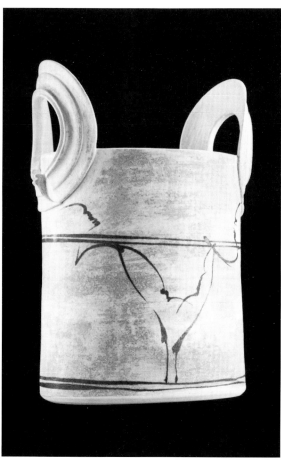

Basket Form, Classical Series 1982
Porcelain, thrown and altered
Multiple glazes, sprayed and brushed
33 × 24 × 16
CMC 86-117 (Bronfman)

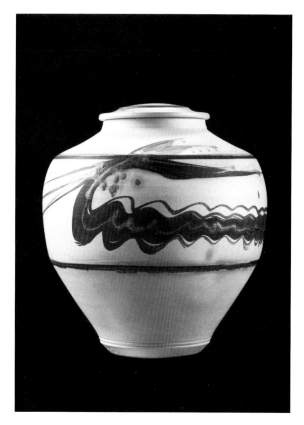

Lidded Jar, Southwest Series 1986
Porcelain, thrown
Terra sigillata, copper and manganese
brushwork, trailed chrome-red glaze
25 × 23 diam.
CMC 86-158.1–2 (Bronfman)

Olympic Mists 1977
Porcelain, slab-built and thrown
Multiple glazes, trailed, poured and
brushed, with added brush decoration
in iron and cobalt oxides; glaze intaglio through wax resist
43 × 25 × 11
CMC 86-112 (Bronfman)

Lidded Jar, Clematis Series 1986
Porcelain, thrown
Multiple glazes, trailed and brushed
42 × 26 diam.
CMC 86-157. 1–2 (Bronfman)

Chronology

1939	Born in Selsdon, Surrey, England
1955	Entered the Croydon College of Art, where he studied drawing and painting, etching, copper and wood engraving, and lithography
1956	Began studying ceramics while continuing work in lithography
1960–65	Studied stage design and scene painting in addition to ceramics and lithography; Graduated from college and worked as an actor, stage designer and director in London's West End theatres
1965	Set up a pottery studio and gallery at Kintbury, Berkshire, England
1965–68	Taught ceramics at the Berkshire College of Art, Reading, Berkshire, England
1968	Immigrated to Canada; Worked as head of ceramics department, Central Technical School, Toronto
1970	Set up a pottery studio and gallery at Hillsdale, Ontario
1970–73	Developed a ceramics and glass department and programme at Georgian College, Barrie, Ontario
1973	Became a full-time studio potter at Hillsdale, Ontario, working with a team of four apprentices
1977	First recipient of the Saidye Bronfman Award for Excellence in the Crafts; Moved to Victoria to establish a new studio and gallery
1978–82	Taught at the Lester B. Pearson College of the Pacific, Victoria; Made a slide presentation of his work at the World Crafts Council Conference in Kyoto, Japan
1983	Began experimenting with landscape murals on ceramic tile; Curated an exhibition, "Ceramic Spectrum", for the Ontario Crafts Council Gallery, Toronto, to coincide with the 1984 publication of his book *The Ceramic Spectrum*
1985–88	Founded the Metchosin International Summer School of the Arts, Victoria, in 1985, and taught courses on ceramic glaze and colour development

Solo Exhibitions

1967	Burford, Oxfordshire, England
1969	Elliot Lake, Ontario
1970, 1975	Canadian Guild of Potters Gallery, Toronto
1974	Ontario Crafts Council Gallery, Toronto; Canadian Gallery, Kingston, Ontario; Hess Gallery, Hamilton, Ontario

1975	House of Ceramics, Vancouver; Canadian Guild of Crafts (Quebec), Montréal		

1975 House of Ceramics, Vancouver; Canadian Guild of Crafts (Quebec), Montréal

1976 Thomas Gallery, Winnipeg; Canadian Gallery, Kingston, Ontario

1977 Thomas Gallery, Winnipeg; Wells Gallery, Ottawa; Rubaiyat Gallery, Calgary

1978–81 "Explorations within a Landscape", a three-year national touring exhibition he organized to acknowledge receipt of the first Saidye Bronfman Award for Excellence in the Crafts

1979 Thomas Gallery, Winnipeg; Rubaiyat Gallery, Calgary

1981 "Exploration within a Classical Theme", Burnaby Art Gallery, Burnaby, British Columbia

1982 Thomas Gallery, Winnipeg; Visual Arts Centre, Montréal

1984 Art Gallery of Greater Victoria, Victoria

1986 Thomas Gallery, Winnipeg; Rubaiyat Gallery, Calgary; Galerie Design en métiers d'art, Québec

1987–89 "Robin Hopper: Ceramic Explorations, 1957–1987", a travelling exhibition co-sponsored by the Koffler Gallery, North York, Ontario, and the Art Gallery of Greater Victoria

Selected Group Exhibitions

1969–70 Canadian Guild of Crafts, Canadian National Exhibition, Toronto; "Craft Dimensions", Royal Ontario Museum, Toronto

1971 "Make", Ontario Science Centre, Toronto

1972 "Canadian Ceramics '72", Royal Ontario Museum, Toronto; Canadian Guild of Crafts, Canadian National Exhibition, Toronto

1973 "Ceramics International '73", Alberta College of Art Gallery, Calgary; organized by the International Ceramic Society, Geneva, Switzerland

1974 "Ontario Master Craftsmen", York University Gallery, Toronto; "Image '74", Art Gallery of Hamilton, Hamilton, Ontario

1976 "Crossroads Invitational", Ontario Crafts Council Gallery, Toronto; "Craft Collaborative", First Canadian Place Gallery, Toronto; "Down to Earth", Ontario Potters Association, Hamilton, Ontario; "National Ceramics", Calgary; "Ceramics in Canada", Koffler Gallery, North York, Ontario

1982 Two-person exhibition, Rembrandt Galleries, North Vancouver

1984 Two-person exhibition, Galerie Poterie Bonsecours, Montréal

Shell Forms, Nos. 5, 1, and 2 1974
Agate porcelain, thrown and altered
Unglazed
Left to right:
No. 5: 20 × 12 diam.
CMC 86-115 (Bronfman)
No. 1: 26 × 14 diam.
CMC 86-113 (Bronfman)
No. 2: 20 × 13 diam.
CMC 86-114 (Bronfman)

Pitcher 1985
Porcelain, thrown
Multiple glazes, poured and sprinkled
with granular ilmenite and rutile
27 × 18 diam.
Lent by the artist

Workshops and Lectures

1973	Waterloo, Toronto, Thunder Bay and Sudbury, Ontario
1975	Calgary; Vancouver; Montréal
1977	Victoria; Edmonton; Yellowknife, Northwest Territories
1978	Vancouver; Halifax; St. John's; Fredericton, New Brunswick; Charlottetown
1981	San Francisco; Conducted a three-month workshop and teaching tour in Australia and New Zealand
1982	Banff Centre, Banff, Alberta; Workshop leader at the Canadian Crafts Council Conference, Charlottetown
1983	Winnipeg; Taught a course in ceramics history and techniques at the Visual Arts Centre, Montréal
1983–84	Conducted a ceramics workshop series in Montréal; Chicago; Columbus, Ohio; Ottawa, Québec, Halifax; and Fairbanks, Alaska
1984	Panelist at the Canadian Clay Conference, Banff, Alberta; Guest lecturer at the Ontario Potters Association Conference, Toronto, and at the Canadian Colour Society Conference, Montréal
1985	Taught a course in ceramics history and techniques at the University of Alaska, Fairbanks, Alaska
1986	Keynote speaker at the Ceramic Symposium in Medicine Hat, Alberta, and the Colour Conference of the International Colour Society in Toronto; Conducted ceramics workshops in San Francisco, Los Angeles and San Diego, California; and in Tucson, Arizona; Moderated the Canadian Crafts Council Conference, Vancouver; Panelist at the Conference of the Canadian Society of Decorative Arts, Victoria
1987	Taught a ceramics glaze and colour course for the Centre de formation et de consultation en métiers d'art, Québec; Conducted ceramics workshops in Calgary, Red Deer and Edmonton, Alberta; and in Dallas and Houston, Texas
1988	Conducted ceramics workshops in Wooster, Ohio, and Louisville, Kentucky

Founder, Member

1969–71	Director at large, Canadian Guild of Crafts; Exhibition chairman, Canadian Guild of Potters
1970–71	Member of the executive, Ontario Craft Foundation (later the Ontario Crafts Council)

1975–77	Founder and first president, Craft Collaborative, Ontario
1978–82	British Columbia representative, Canadian Crafts Council
1979–82	Founding member and first president, Ceramists Canada
1984	Founder and first president, Metchosin International Summer School of the Arts, Victoria

Selected Publications

1970	"Glazemaking Simplified", a series of technical articles for *Tactile* magazine, published by the Canadian Guild of Potters
1975	"Glazemaking Simplified" and "Ceramic Colour Development", articles written for *Ceramic Review* (England)
1982	Completed research and wrote *The Ceramic Spectrum*, published in 1984
1984	Wrote and illustrated *Functional Pottery*, published in 1986
1985	"Roots, Growth, Rhythm and Balance: The Working Potter", *Studio Potter* 13, no. 2: 25–27
1987–89	Wrote *Making Marks: Discovering the Decorated Ceramic Surface*, to be published in 1990
1988	Wrote a series of articles on glaze and colour development, to be published in *Ceramics Monthly*

Television and Film

1973	Was the subject of a one-hour television programme on ceramics, Thunder Bay, Ontario
1974	Featured potter in the educational film *Introduction to Pottery*, produced for use at high-school and college levels by Morteland-Latchford, Toronto
1982–83	Consultant, host and narrator of "Glorious Mud", a one-hour television programme on ceramics produced for the CBC series, Hand and Eye; first shown in February 1984

Lois Etherington Betteridge

The work of Lois Betteridge bears witness to the classical tradition of silversmithing. The making of beautiful objects for special and important functions signifies the celebration of ritual and the honouring of culture. This is Lois Betteridge's stated purpose and the reason that her work speaks so strongly to us. Further, the making of beautiful objects for simple, everyday use elevates their use to the status of ritual and, in the silversmith's words, "extends the role of precious objects beyond mere function." This is the romanticizing of the utilitarian object. To imbue it with a spiritual presence and to give it elegance and specialness is to allow it to create an environment in which usefulness becomes an accolade and symbolism a direct attribute of the human touch.

Silver has been considered a precious material as far back as human history can be traced. Its brilliant sheen and ability to be worked into detailed and refined forms has afforded it a secure place in the fine-artisan's repertoire of materials. It is particularly suited to the sensibility of Lois Betteridge's work. Hers is work that is sensuous and decorative. Objects have been materialized into harmonious forms. Parts of the whole flow into one another, and transitions are marked with fine detail. Accents of additional materials are sparingly used, and serve to enhance the richness of the master material. Such a refined use of silver evokes the idea of Beauty.

The concept of an idealized form has been pursued and reassessed since at least as far back as Classical Greece. But the rather cool, rarefied results are not always satisfactory. Thus the idea of Beauty as emotion and feeling, as touchable, and perhaps therefore more human, strikes a responsive chord. The work of Lois Betteridge follows this approach. Whether her individual romantic pieces take organic or geometric forms, they are essentially emotional. They deal with the connection of our feelings to the world around us. They speak to us and the world through their use in celebrations, whether those celebrations are of a formal or a private nature.

The object that is made to fulfil a specific purpose reaches its completion when it is finally used. Thus, Lois Betteridge carefully and thoughtfully structures every nuance of her work toward the act of use and the pleasures of recognizing its symbolic content. Its relationship to use, ritual and celebration, and to all aspects of its decoration and form speak of touch and feeling. The romantic connection is made. It is with this approach to Beauty that Lois Betteridge creates a harmonious unity of object and function.

Technical excellence, perfection if you will, must also be present. It is the mark of fine artisanry. It is the human touch made visible and the formal manifestation of Beauty. Lois Betteridge's work is second to none. Exquisitely finished surfaces, attention to the smallest details, consideration for every angle of view, and elegant nuances of technique characterize her objects. Hers is master craftsmanship at its highest level.

A final aspect of the tradition of artisanry, and one that tends to be overlooked today, is the slow and measured unfolding of style that is the core of a life's work. For this reason it is comforting and enlightening to see the various manifestations of Lois Betteridge's unfolding approach to style. Her work may be organic or geometric in form, serious or playful in intent, but it has a particular approach to relationships of size and shape, a definite preference for a range of scale, a clear attitude toward functional elegance, and a strong relationship to symbol and meaning. It has a unique hand.

Carole Hanks
Teacher of art and design history
Sheridan College
Oakville, Ontario

Box for Woodwind Reed 1982
Sterling silver
Constructed
9.0 × 4.1 × 3.5
CMC 86-103.1–2 (Bronfman)

Chronology

1928	Born in Drummondville, Quebec
1948–49	Attended foundation year at the Ontario College of Art, Toronto
1951	Graduated with a Bachelor of Fine Arts degree from the University of Kansas, Lawrence, Kansas
1952	Moved from Kansas to Oakville, Ontario, and opened her first studio, returning one year later to Toronto; supplemented her income from metalwork sales by teaching jewellery making in community classes
1954–56	Granted a scholarship to study metalsmithing at the Cranbrook Academy of Art, Bloomfield Hills, Michigan, graduating in 1956 with a Master of Fine Arts degree
1957–60	Moved to Guelph, Ontario, to teach design, jewellery making, weaving and woodworking at the Ontario Agricultural College
1960	Married, resigned her teaching position, but continued to use the College metal studio to complete several ecclesiastical commissions
1961–67	Moved with her husband to England, where she experimented with lead and the lost-wax technique of metal casting and developed her silversmithing aesthetic; had two children
1967–80	Moved with her family to Ottawa, where she set up a studio, and continued to accept commissions for jewellery, ecclesiastical silver and secular hollow-ware; Exhibited widely, taught, and served on exhibition juries
1978	Second recipient of the Saidye Bronfman Award for Excellence in the Crafts
1980	Moved near Mont-Saint-Hilaire, Quebec, and re-established her studio
1985	Moved to Guelph, Ontario, again establishing a studio

Selected Solo Exhibitions

1971	Wells Gallery, Ottawa
1973	Algonquin College, Ottawa
1978	Eaton's Art Gallery, Eaton Centre, Toronto
1981	Alberta College of Art, Calgary; Capilano College, North Vancouver; Ontario Crafts Council Gallery, Toronto
1982	University of Waterloo, Waterloo, Ontario; London Regional Art Gallery, London, Ontario; National Exhibition Centre, Fredericton, New Brunswick; Mount Saint Vincent University, Halifax

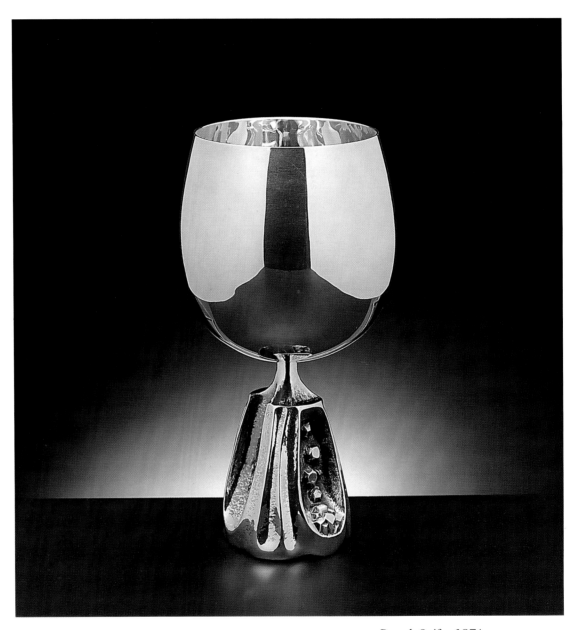

Brandy Snifter 1974
Sterling silver, synthetic emerald,
baroque pearl
Raised, chased, repoussé, fabricated,
cast, set
20.3 × 11.0 diam.
CMC 86-101 (Bronfman)

Private Communion Set 1965
Sterling silver
Raised, fabricated
Fitted wooden box by H.M. Forster,
Ruislip, Middlesex, England:
20.4 × 20.2 × 20.1
CMC 86-104.1–11
Gift of the artist

1983	National Museum of Natural Sciences, Ottawa; Yaneff Gallery, Toronto	1969	"Contemporary Jewellery", Sheridan College of Applied Arts and Technology, Mississauga, Ontario; "Craft Dimensions Canada", Royal Ontario Museum, Toronto; "Canadian Guild of Crafts", Canadian National Exhibition, Toronto
1984	Stewart Hall Art Gallery, Pointe-Claire, Quebec		
1987	Georgian College of Applied Arts and Technology, Barrie, Ontario		
1988	Art Gallery of Hamilton, Hamilton, Ontario	1969–73	Six travelling exhibitions for the Ontario Department of Education, Toronto

Selected Group Exhibitions

1951	"Annual Craft Show", Wichita Art Association, Wichita, Kansas	1970	Canadian Pavilion and the Commissioner General's suite, Expo 70, Osaka, Japan
1952	"Craftsman Show", Canadian National Exibition, Toronto	1975	"Survey Exhibition", Visual Arts Ottawa, Ottawa; "Art in Craft", Canadian Guild of Crafts, Toronto
1956	"Michigan Artists-Craftsmen", Michigan Craftsmen's Association, Detroit		
1957	"Crafts – Past and Present", Canadian Handicrafts Guild, Toronto	1978	"Artisan 78", national travelling exhibition, Canadian Crafts Council, Ottawa
1963	"Jewellery '63", State University College at Plattsburgh, New York	1978–79	"Métiers d'Art 3", invitational exhibition, Canadian cultural centres in Paris, Strasbourg, Brussels, London
1964–65	"Thames Valley Artists", Thames Valley Artists' Association, London		
1966	"De Beers International Ring Competitions", De Beers Consolidated Mines Limited, London	1980	"Mug Shots", Holland College of Applied Arts and Technology, Charlottetown
1966–67	"Crafts", Craft Centre of Great Britain, London	1982	"The Michigan Influence", Eastern Michigan University, Ypsilanti, Michigan
1967	"Ten Canadian Abstract Artists Overseas", Edinburgh Festival, Edinburgh	1985	"Grand Prix des Métiers d'Art", Montréal

1987	"Fidem Eighty-Seven, USA", Fédération internationale de la médaille, Colorado Springs, Colorado; "Metalworks", Cranbrook Academy of Art Museum, Bloomfield Hills, Michigan	1958	Marymount College, Sudbury, Ontario
		1964	Arnolfini Gallery, Bristol, England
		1965	E.A. Kelsey, Stroud, England
		1969	Sheridan College of Applied Arts and Technology, Mississauga, Ontario
1988	"Masters of American Metal-smithing", Schering-Plough corporate headquarters, Madison, New Jersey; "Hallowed Objects", provincial touring exhibition, Ontario Crafts Council Gallery, Toronto; "Spatial Inclinations: Architectural Influences", organized by the Metal Arts Guild, shown at the Ontario Crafts Council Gallery, Toronto; "Grand Prix des Métiers d'Art", Montréal; Royal Canadian Academy of Arts, inaugural exhibition, Academy House, Toronto; "Ontario Metalsmiths", Städtisches Museum,Schwäbisch Gmünd, West Germany; "Lois Etherington Betteridge: Recent Works", Art Gallery of Hamilton, Hamilton, Ontario	1970	Gift for the Right Honourable Pierre Elliott Trudeau commissioned by the Liberal caucus
		1973	Ontario Crafts Council, Toronto
		1974	Christ Church Cathedral, Vancouver; International Business Machines, Ottawa
		1976	Canadian Crafts Council, Ottawa
		1977	Joan A. Chalmers National Craft Collection, Toronto
		1978	National Museum of Natural Sciences, Ottawa
		1980	Imperial Oil of Canada, Ottawa; Canadian Museum of Civilization, Massey Foundation Collection
		1981	Canadian Pacific, Montréal
		1983	McLuhan Teleglobe Canada Award, Ottawa; Cranbrook Art Gallery, Bloomfield Hills, Michigan

Selected Commissions and Collections

1953	Toronto-Dominion Bank, Sudbury, Ontario	1984	*Bringing the Constitution Home*, presented to the Right Honourable Pierre Elliott Trudeau by the Peace by Peace People of Canada
1954, 1960	St. Christopher's Anglican Church, Burlington, Ontario	1986	International Symposium on Equine Reproduction, Calgary

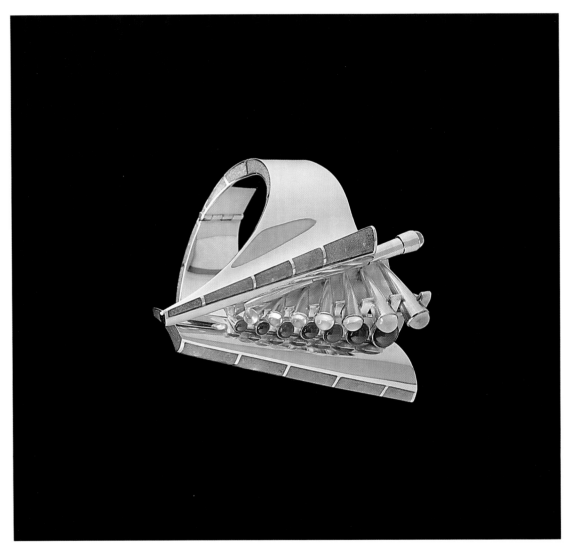

Bracelet 1976
Sterling silver, moonstone, British
Columbia jade, Quebec serpentine
Fabricated, inlaid, set
23.5 × 10.9
Lent by the National Museum of
Natural Sciences, Ottawa

Script Assistant 1977
Sterling silver, soapstone, gold pen-
nib
Raised, chased, constructed, carved
Bottle: 16.9 × 8.2 diam.
Pen: 18.7 × 1.2 diam.
Stand: 18.5 × 14.9 × 2.4
CMC 86-102.1–3 (Bronfman)

1987	Department of External Affairs, Ottawa	1977, 1985, 1987	New Brunswick Craft School, Fredericton, New Brunswick; School of Visual Arts, Charlotte-town; Sydney Metal Smiths, Sydney, Nova Scotia; University of Michigan, Ann Arbor, Michigan; The Michigan Silversmiths' Guild, Detroit; Centre for Creative Studies, College of Art and Design, Detroit
1988	Canadian Museum of Civilization, Samuel and Saidye Bronfman Family Foundation Collection		

Teaching and Workshops

1952–54	Ryerson Polytechnical Institute, Toronto		
1954–56	Ontario Board of Education, Community Programmes Branch, Georgetown, Ontario		
1957–60	Ontario Agricultural College, Macdonald Institute, Guelph, Ontario	1978	Glasgow College of Art, Glasgow, Scotland
1973–74	Mohawk College of Applied Arts and Technology, Hamilton, Ontario	1980–82	L'atelier de joaillerie, Montréal
		1981	Concordia University, Faculty of Fine Arts, Montréal
1972, 1975	Sheridan College of Applied Arts and Technology, Mississauga, Ontario	1981–88	Ontario College of Art, Toronto; Haliburton Summer School of Fine Arts, Haliburton, Ontario
1971, 1974, 1977, 1981, 1987	Nova Scotia College of Art and Design, Halifax	1982	First Canadian Crafts Conference, Halifax
1974, 1976–78	Algonquin College of Applied Arts and Technology, Ottawa	1988	Metal Arts Guild, Toronto; Sheffield City Polytechnic, Sheffield, England; Edinburgh College of Art, Edinburgh

Selected Publications

1958	"The Function of the Artist in Canada", *Ontario Agricultural College Review and Alumni News*, pp. 8–9

| 1975 | "The Technique of Chasing and Repoussé", *Crafts Canada* 1, no. 2: 26–29 |
| 1978 | "Lois Betteridge, an Autobiography", *Goldsmiths Journal* 17, no. 2: 30–31 |

Selected Television and Radio

1970	"Women in Art", Canadian Women Artists Series, CBC national radio
1976	"The Arts", CBC national television
1978	"Arts National", CBC radio
1984	"Morningside", interview with Peter Gzowski, 6 February, CBC national radio; "All That Glistens", Hand and Eye Series, CBC national television

Honours and Awards

1954	Helen Scripps Booth Scholarship for graduate studies, Cranbrook Academy of Art, Bloomfield Hills, Michigan
1974	Elected Distinguished Member, Society of North American Goldsmiths
1975	Citation for distinguished professional achievement, University of Kansas, Lawrence, Kansas
1978	Elected Member, Royal Canadian Academy of Arts
1988	Fellowship of the New Brunswick Craft School, Fredericton, New Brunswick

Wild Flowers 1981
Cotton cloth
Quilted, appliquéd, embroidered
279 × 234
CMC 86-144
Gift of Ann Mortimer

I find it difficult to believe that I met Monique Cliche-Spénard over twenty years ago. She has not changed in her love of anecdote, in her determination to bring to a conclusion every undertaking she believes in, and in her struggle to defend every just cause, whether it be artistic, cultural, political or social.

Her philosophy of life is one that has enabled her to face adversity and to emerge stronger and with more vitality than ever. For this reason, working at her side is not a task but a pleasure. Her openness fosters the atmosphere essential to creativity, and encourages a close collaboration that leads to productive results. Her great zest for life, combined with a deep love of the past, makes her sensitive to everything in her surroundings. Always open to the suggestions of others, she is equally ready to share her own ideas, and hours of work quickly become hours of pleasure devoted to a common creation. The friendship that grows from this type of relationship endures forever.

Having gone through difficult times early in life, Monique now surrounds herself with a group of women who will give her support, assistance in her work, and love, an emotion she returns generously. This atmosphere of friendship lends the work produced at the Atelier Monique Cliche-Spénard that air of freshness and beauty that used to be found in the quilting of our grandmothers.

Monique's first experiments in oil painting soon led her into adult education, where she quickly made contact with interesting people in various communities of the Beauce region. Her already marked interest in tradition intensified. A collector for several years, she acquired more and more antiques (from which she would later borrow intriguing motifs) and, increasingly, delved deeper into their history. It was in this way that she rediscovered quilting and set out to show the endless possibilities it offered.

With her undeniable love of drawing and the ordering of colours, Monique worked to bring new vitality to the art of quilting and to make it so attractive that it would blend with any decor, modern or traditional, because of its varied tones and dimensions.

The source of inspiration for her much-admired creations is her home region of the Beauce. Monique transforms the features that have characterized the region for over a century into a harmony of shapes and colours, and gives them new vibrancy by her careful choice of fabrics. Her Beauce landscapes make us want to see and know more; this is what she considers her personal contribution to the region.

Monique has accomplished the task she set herself of reviving a tradition and introducing it not only to countless Quebec homes but across Canada and abroad. She has rekindled people's love of the past in a form that is novel, beautiful and useful. Because of Monique, quilting is once again a part of everyday life, whether the finished product is signed by Cliche-Spénard or another agile hand.

There need be no fear of any decline in the work of Monique Cliche-Spénard. Her creativity, constantly on the boil, is always ready to burst forth with new designs. They may surprise us, but are guaranteed to be both interesting and strikingly beautiful.

Luce Bernard
Placer gold miner
Dawson, Yukon Territory

The Cabin at Saint-Zacharie 1979
Cotton cloth
Quilted, appliquéd
119 × 80
CMC 86-140
Gift of Ann Mortimer

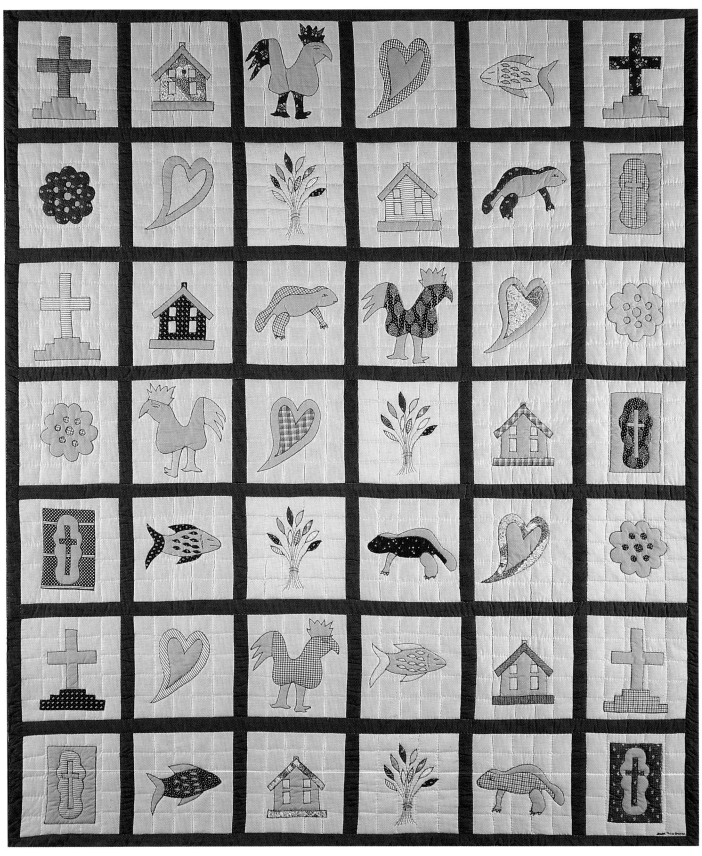

Sugar Moulds 1974
Cotton cloth
Quilted, appliquéd
269 × 229
CMC 86-133
Gift of Ann Mortimer

The Heart of the Village 1977
Cotton cloth
Quilted, appliquéd
230 × 202
CMC 86-126
Gift of Ann Mortimer

Chronology

1926	Born in Saint-Joseph-de-Beauce, Quebec
1934–41	Attended primary school at the Sisters of Charity convent in Saint-Joseph-de-Beauce
1939	Death of her mother, Béatrice Gosselin
1944–45	Attended secondary school at the Ursuline convent in Québec
1946–47	Studied domestic science at La Ruche school in Québec
1949	Married Gérard Spénard at the Québec Basilica
1958	Gérard Spénard injured at work in Sorel, Quebec
1959	Moved to Saint-Georges in the Beauce region
1960–70	Met with women from the Beauce region and elsewhere to catalogue the various patterns used in quilting
1964–67	Studied oil painting at the school of arts and crafts in Saint-Georges, Quebec
1969	Death of her father, Léonce Cliche; Gérard Spénard family moved to Saint-Joseph-de-Beauce
1971–73	Taught traditional and popular art in the Beauce region of Quebec
1972	Studied high-warp tapestry at the Moulin des Arts in Saint-Étienne-de-Lauzon, Quebec
1973	Began quilting at Saint-Joseph-de-Beauce
1974	Created the quilt *Sugar Moulds*
1975	Founded the Atelier Monique Cliche-Spénard at Saint-Joseph-de-Beauce
1976–77	Quilting instructor for the Commission scolaire of the Eastern Townships
1979	Third recipient of the Saidye Bronfman Award for Excellence in the Crafts; Created the quilt *Vitaline*
1980	Chosen a Person of the Year for achieving exceptional success in her profession and for her contribution to improving the status of women, Salon de la Femme, Montréal
1983–85	Opened a summer boutique, La Maison des Artisans, in Saint-Joseph-de-Beauce
1986	Instructor for a group of English students at the Séminaire Saint-Georges-de-Beauce

Selected Solo Exhibitions

1976	Manoir Couillard-Dupuis, Montmagny, Quebec
1977	Town Hall, Saint-Georges, Quebec; Gallery of the Corporation des artisans de Québec, Québec
1979	Boutique La Courtisane, Québec; Exhibitions in France at Dunkirk, Grenoble, Nancy, and Annecy
1980	Baie-Saint-Paul Art Centre, Baie-Saint-Paul, Québec; Manoir de Tonnancour, Pointe-du-Lac, Quebec

1981	Visual Arts Centre, Montréal
1982	Domaine-Forget music academy, Saint-Irénée, Quebec; University of Toronto, Toronto; Centre d'Activités françaises, Penetanguishene, Ontario
1984	Musée Marius Barbeau, Saint-Joseph-de-Beauce, Quebec; Galerie d'Art L'Heureux, Trois-Rivières, Quebec
1986	Benedict Arnold Hotel, Saint-Georges, Quebec

Selected Group Exhibitions

1970, 1980	Caisse populaire de Saint-Joseph-de-Beauce, Quebec
1974	Salon de la Femme du Québec, Québec
1976–84	Salon des Métiers d'art du Québec, Montréal
1977–78	Festival of Spring, Ottawa
1977–80, 1982	Salon des Artisans de Québec, Québec
1978	Member of the Quebec delegation to the Metro Toronto International Caravan, as representative of the Centrale d'artisanat du Québec
1980	Lévis Art Centre, Lévis, Quebec
1982	YMCA, Montréal; Salon des Arts, Méridien Hotel, Montréal
1985–88	"One of a Kind", Toronto
1987	Town Hall, Saint-Georges, Quebec; Polyvalente de Saint-Joseph-de-Beauce, Quebec; Édifice "G", Gouvernement du Québec, Québec

| 1988 | City Hall, Chartres, France; Boutique Le Noeud, Baie-Saint-Paul, Quebec; Musée Sartigan, Saint-Georges, Quebec |

Memberships

Active member of the Salon des Métiers d'art du Québec
Active member of the Corporation des artisans de Québec
Active member of the Société du Patrimoine des Beaucerons
Member of the Canadian Crafts Council since 1977
Member of the Conseil de la Culture de la Région de Québec since 1980

Television

| 1977 | Participated in "Le fil du temps" [The Thread of Time], the second part of a film entitled "Courtepointe" [Quilting], by Marcel G. Sabourin |

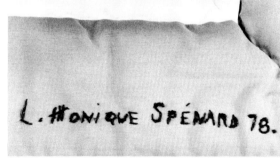

My first memorable impression of Louise Doucet and Satoshi Saito dates from the mid-sixties. They had rented a house in North Hatley, Quebec, and had invited a number of friends for dinner. The power failed. Louise quietly poured more wine. Satoshi rushed bowls and trays of mysteriously prepared fish, fowl, rice and seaweed to the Pottery on the other side of the village, which still had electricity. Within the hour, without apparent fuss, East joined West in a candlelit Japanese-style dinner.

I was impressed again, several years later, when I brought home a pair of Doucet–Saito pitchers. They serenely declared the other pitcher in the house to be a shoddily glazed impostor. It was an instant education.

Today, as I drive up to their white farmhouse overlooking the village of Ways Mills, Quebec, the neighbour's cows merely stare, the old yellow Lab doesn't even lift his head, and the potting shed at the end of his run looks as though it might hold lawn chairs put away for the winter. Only the wind disturbs a pile of raked leaves. Simplicity, order, silence belie two decades of activity: planting the garden, travelling to Japan, raising three children, wresting clay from a Nova Scotia quarry, and creating hundreds of artifacts – from tiny sake cups to a free-standing granite sculpture almost the size of the potting shed and some tons heavier.

That activity begins to be manifest when Louise appears, then Satoshi, and we walk around to the front of the house. Various silent figures inhabit the lawn, their glazed surfaces reflecting the greys, pinks and rusts of the late-

October landscape. But the light is engaged in an unexpectedly dynamic game. Rhomboids, doubly or triply warped, join in sensuous and sometimes razor-edged seams to form solids, one resting intimately, but not precisely, on the other.

Sculpture 1980
Stoneware
37 × 21 × 20
Lent by Mrs. Sharon Schwartz

The work of Doucet–Saito is neither sensational nor arbitrary. It has evolved year by year, in effect exploring all the possibilities of the slab: multiplied horizontally, it becomes a mosaic; layered vertically, it becomes a style; joined in three dimensions, it becomes an urn, a vase, a torso, which may then be opened, unfolded, split like a cell. Throughout, there is a play of textures and forms, of inside and outside, of the yin and the yang.

Radically scuptural, theirs is an art realized through the hands – a bodily synthesis of knowledge and desire. The initially flexible clay has been central to its development. Increasingly, however, they have explored other materials – wood, stone, metal – and they have managed adjustments in scale, from the domestic to the monumental, their work finding a place in the lives, not only of individuals, but of public institutions – even a police station.

Inside, we sit around the table, eating small cylinders of rice wrapped in black seaweed and topped with a brilliant pink roe. Satoshi talks of two months' work preparing optional designs and mock-ups for a 12-metre mural in a new building. Neither design won budget approval. Ways Mills, I think, has been an ideal place to work and grow, but now it may provide limited opportunities to realize the manifold possibilities of a fully mature art. I am haunted by the great dancing rift in one of the proposed designs, unrealized. Yet I am also haunted by a 60-centimetre ceramic piece, something between the idea of a castle keep and a Corbusier,

ghostly but real on the pine cupboard, just behind my back, in the corner. It is actual, and alive.

D.G. Jones
Professor of English
Université de Sherbrooke
Sherbrooke, Quebec

Vase 1966
Stoneware, unglazed
26 × 26 × 21
Lent by the artists

Sculpture 1985
Stoneware
41 × 37 × 31
CMC 86-97 (Bronfman)

Sculpture 1976
Stoneware
54 × 33 × 18
Lent by External Affairs Canada

Sculpture 1975
Stoneware
44 × 29 diam.
Lent by External Affairs Canada

Sculpture 1982
Stoneware
32 × 21 × 19
Lent by the Musée du Québec,
Québec

Sculpture 1980
Stoneware
32 × 31 × 15
Lent by Ann Mortimer

Chronology

Satoshi Saito

1935	Born in Tokyo
1957–61	Studied economics at Keio University, Tokyo
1961–64	Graduate studies in economics at McGill University, Montréal
1963	Began working in the studio with Louise Doucet
1965–67	Studied Oriental ceramics in Japan with Tatsuzo Shimaoka and Seimei and Kyo Tsuji

Louise Doucet Saito

1938	Born in Montréal
1957–60	Studied at the School of Art and Design, Montreal Museum of Fine Arts, and majored in sculpture; Took evening course in ceramics for two years at the École du Meuble, Montréal
1961	Rented a studio in North Hatley, Quebec, and worked with Gaétan Beaudin for two years
1963	Began working with Satoshi Saito in the studio
1965	Received a Canada Council grant to study in Japan
1965–67	With Satoshi Saito studied Oriental ceramics in Japan with Tatsuzo Shimaoka and Seimei and Kyo Tsuji

Doucet–Saito

1967	Returned to Canada
1971	Undertook the building of their own kiln in Ways Mills, Quebec, where they still live and work
1980	Fourth recipients of the Saidye Bronfman Award for Excellence in the Crafts

Selected Solo Exhibitions

1965	Canadian Guild of Crafts (Quebec), Montréal
1966	Tochigi Culture Centre, Utsunomiya, Japan
1967, 1976	Matsuya Gallery, Tokyo
1972, 1973, 1975	Canadian Guild of Crafts (Quebec), Montréal
1978	Meitetsu Gallery, Nagoya, Japan
1980	Canadian Guild of Crafts (Quebec), Montréal
1981	Orford Art Centre, Magog, Quebec; Caisse populaire de Sherbrooke-Est, Sherbrooke, Quebec
1982	Art Gallery at Harbourfront, Toronto; Fava Gallery, Oberlin, Ohio
1983	Le Musée du Saguenay–Lac-Saint-Jean, Chicoutimi, Quebec
1985	Koffler Gallery, Toronto; Fourth International Ceramics Symposium, Toronto
1987	Ufundi Gallery, Ottawa

Selected Group Exhibitions

1963	"Canadian Ceramics '63", a national travelling exhibition
1965	"Canadian Ceramics '65", a national travelling exhibition
1967	Canadian Pavilion, Expo 67, Montréal
1976	Centre culturel canadien, Paris; Travelling exhibition in Europe; "Faces of Canada", Canadian Guild of Crafts (Quebec), Québec and Montréal
1978	"Artisan '78", Canadian Crafts Council
1979	"Shigaraki: 800 Years of Clay and Fire", Isetan Museum, Tokyo
1982	Fortieth "Concorso Internazionale della Ceramica d'Arte", Faenza, Italy
1983	"Universiades '83", Edmonton
1988	Olympic Arts Festival, Calgary

Selected Commissions

1978	Mural, Quebec Provincial Police Building, Sherbrooke, Quebec; Design and fabrication of a silver medallion for the Prix du Québec
1982	Mural, Centre local de services communautaires de la Chaumière, Asbestos, Quebec
1983	Stone sculpture, private collection, Oakville, Ontario
1984	Mural, Imperial Life Assurance Company of Canada, Toronto; Fireplace, residence of the Governor General of Canada, The Citadel, Québec
1985	Outside brick wall of gymnasium, Saint-Jean-Baptiste School, Roxton Falls, Quebec
1986	Brass sculpture, Foyer Sacré-Coeur, Magog, Quebec; Ticket office, Orford Art Centre, Magog, Quebec; Mural, Camp musical d'Asbestos, Asbestos, Quebec
1988	Work on granite, Maison du Granit, Lac-Drolet, Quebec

Teaching and Workshops

1980	Banff Centre, School of Fine Arts, Banff, Alberta
1982	Artists-in-residence, Oberlin College, Oberlin, Ohio

Awards

1963	Concours artistique de la Province de Québec, second prize; Functional Design Prize, Government of Canada Design Contest
1973	Marjorie Durnford Award, Canadian Guild of Crafts (Quebec)
1975	Award of excellence, Canadian Guild of Crafts (Quebec)
1976	Donald Dow Award, Canadian Guild of Crafts (Quebec)
1982, 1983	Bourse de la Province de Québec for research in ceramics

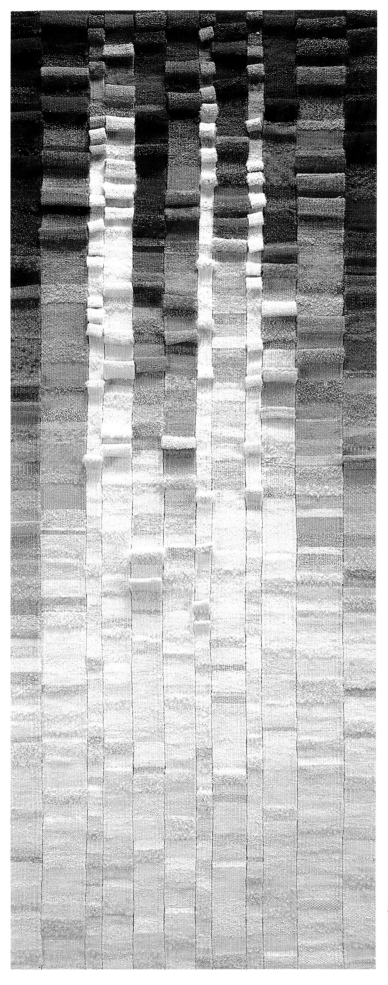

Blue Cascade 1981
Wool, silk, mohair and cotton fibres
Woven, glued
243 × 97
CMC 86-9 (Bronfman)

Baffles 1981
Wool, silk, mohair and cotton fibres
Woven, stitched
170 × 168
Lent by Mr. and Mrs. Charles
Bronfman

In the early 1970s, when I was curator of the Merton Gallery in Toronto, I remember seeing a small, finely woven tapestry in muted golds, reds and purples. It was in the annual juried exhibition of the Ontario Crafts Council. The work of Joanna Staniszkis of Vancouver, it was sophisticated in design and execution, original, and obviously created by a promising artist. I invited her to join the expanding group of fibre artists showing at the Merton Gallery, and a year later she had her first Toronto exhibition. We did not meet until the day Joanna arrived in her station wagon with her husband Tom, baby son Michael, their three-legged dog, and the complete exhibition rolled up in the back of the wagon.

By her second exhibition at the Merton Gallery, in 1974, Joanna and I were meeting with public and corporate clients in hospitals, cemeteries and boardrooms to discuss commissions for tapestries for architectural spaces. Joanna's training as an interior designer and her long association with architects made her a perfect catalyst for the creation of this type of art.

I particularly remember one project, a nine-metre-high tapestry. She created it in Toronto in 1976 for the Government of the Yukon Territory, and wove it in an old downtown warehouse. A section of the floor was removed along the wall to allow the warp to ascend through to the room above. A trestle, holding Joanna, her assistant and baskets of colourful wools and silks, was placed in front of the warp and slowly raised from the first to the second floor as the work progressed. Subsequently, suspended from the large front wall of the Merton Gallery, the tapestry was photographed from the far end of a parking lot, the only way to make a record of the large work before it was sent to Whitehorse.

My role as coordinator was fascinating and challenging, for large woven tapestries were new to Toronto and to me. Joanna showed me how these works, designed for a given space, require consideration in installation, lighting and maintenance. They must float against the wall, the shadow around the form creating a frame, and lighting must be from an angle to highlight the texture of the piece.

There is another important facet to Joanna's personality. In my collection of well-worn hats is a cloche she made especially for me. It is crocheted of brown wool with yellow, orange and red trim, designed to brighten dreary Toronto winters. Joanna also has a hat collection – remarkable hats gathered around the world at market stalls or through colleagues. They reflect a personal study of the design and function of headgear from the past and the present. Displayed on walls and shelves, protected in drawers and boxes in her home and studio are the other textiles in her collection. They include fragments of ancient weavings from South America, fine white woven and embroidered Victorian linens and cottons, and exquisite kimonos from Japan.

Joanna is a serious student of textiles, with a passionate interest in folk art. The language of the weaver possesses a rich and diverse vocabulary, which she explores for inspiration and

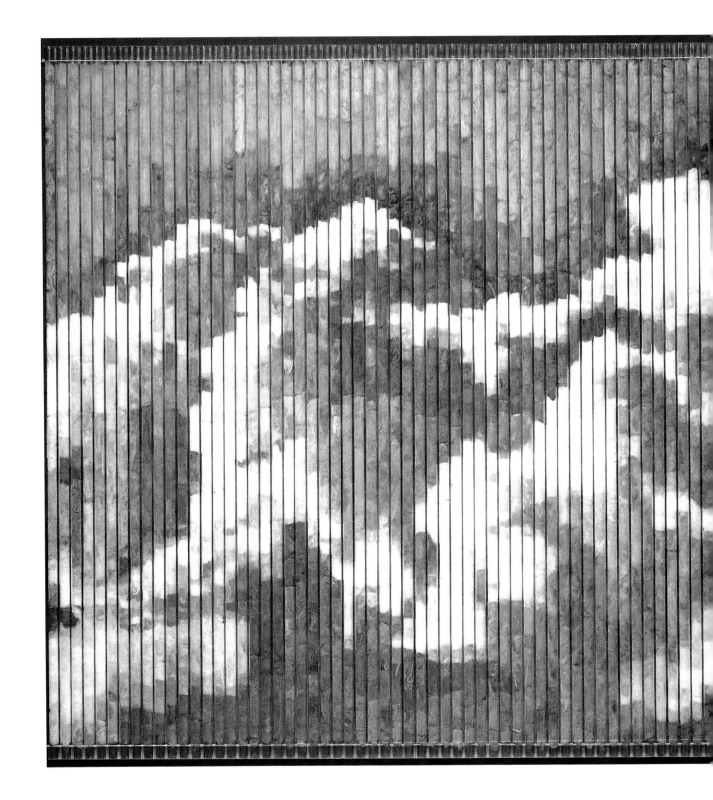

Cloudscape 1985
Wool, raw silk and synthetic fibres,
Plexiglas tubes
Dyed, stuffed, assembled
366 × 183
CMC 86-124 (Bronfman)

understanding. A natural and enthusiastic communicator, she combines research with teaching during holiday trips she organizes to museums in South America or the Far East for her design students at the University of British Columbia.

That small finely woven tapestry, which now hangs in an office of the Ontario Crafts Council, reminds me of the special person whose talent both supports and inspires and whose friendship has been so important to me.

Jean Johnson
Coordinator
The Craft Studio at Harbourfront
Toronto

Chronology

1944	Born in Poland
1962–64	Studied at the Fine Arts Academy, Warsaw
1964–67	Received a United States Department of State scholarship to study at the Art Institute of Chicago; graduated with an Honours Bachelor of Fine Arts degree
1966	Studied pre-Columbian textiles in Lima, Peru
1969–89	Joined the School of Home Economics, University of British Columbia, as a design instructor; developed the design programme and continues to teach as an associate professor of design
1975	Travelled to Bolivia, Peru and Ecuador to study pre-Columbian textiles
1975–76	Acting head of the textile design department, Ontario College of Art, Toronto
1978	Studied contemporary Bolivian costume in Bolivia
1980	Elected to the Royal Canadian Academy of Arts
1981	Fifth recipient of the Saidye Bronfman Award for Excellence in the Crafts
1981, 1983	Received the Dean's Grant, University of British Columbia, to study contemporary Bolivian costume and headgear in Bolivia
1982–83	Took a sabbatical leave to study at Aix-en-Provence, France
1984–88	Study trips to Thailand, Burma, Hong Kong, Nepal, India, and Indonesia

Selected Solo Exhibitions

1972, 1974, 1976	Merton Gallery, Toronto
1973	Mido Framers Gallery, Vancouver
1978	Equinox Gallery, Vancouver
1979	University of British Columbia, Faculty Club, Vancouver
1988	Cartwright Street Gallery, Vancouver
1989	University of British Columbia, Museum of Anthropology, Vancouver

Selected Group Exhibitions

1973–74	"Textiles into 3-D", a travelling exhibition organized by the Art Gallery of Ontario, Toronto
1976	International Tapestry Exhibition, Vevey, Switzerland; Tapestry exhibition, Art Gallery of Windsor, Windsor, Ontario
1976–77	International tapestry exhibition, Jacques Baruch Gallery, Chicago
1976, 1978, 1981, 1985	International Tapestry Triennial, Lodz, Poland
1980	Royal Canadian Academy of Arts, Centennial exhibition, Toronto

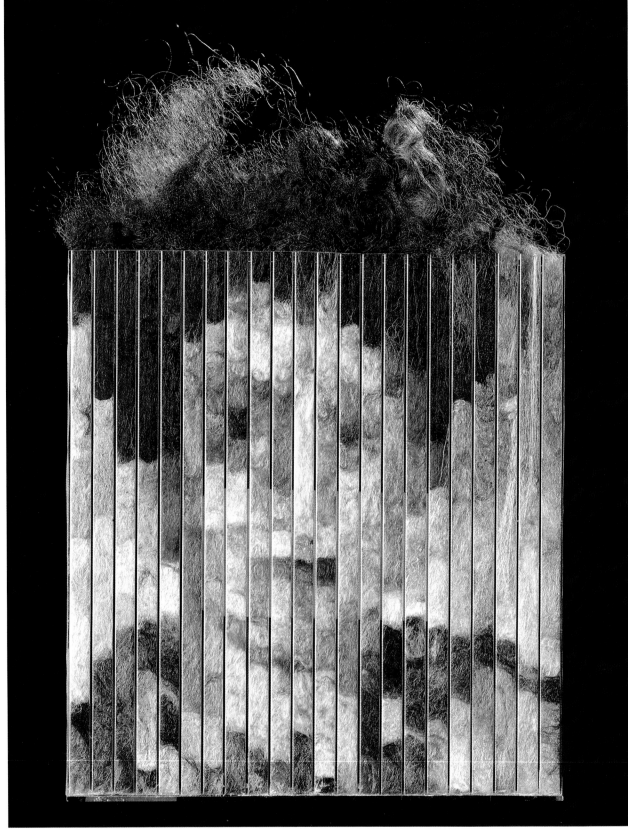

Hairy 1985–86
Wool and synthetic fibres, Plexiglas channels
Dyed, stuffed, assembled
23 × 15
Lent by the artist

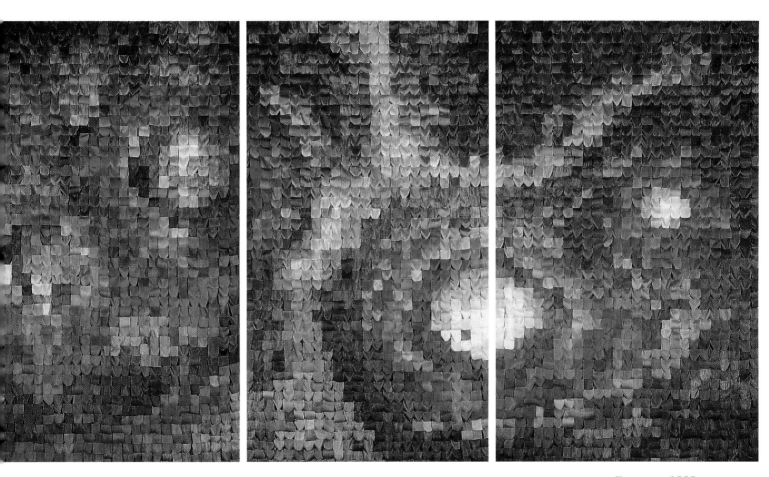

Fragments 1988
Parachute silk, nylon fishnet
Cut, dyed, assembled
408 × 187
Lent by the artist

1981–83	"Gregor, Rousseau-Vermette and Staniszkis", a national travelling exhibition organized by the Art Gallery of Windsor, Windsor, Ontario
1986	"Artists in Space – Fibre", F.I.T. Gallery, New York

Selected Architectural Commissions

1973	Mount Pleasant Cemetery Memorial Chapel, Toronto; Bank of Montreal, Bentall III Building, Vancouver
1975	Laurel Medical Centre, Vancouver; International Plaza Hotel, Vancouver; Sunnybrook Hospital, Veterans Wing, Toronto
1975, 1981	Westcoast Transmission Company, Vancouver
1976	Yukon Territorial Building, Whitehorse, Yukon Territory; *Toronto Star* Building, Toronto
1977	Polish embassy, Tokyo; Alberta Gas Trunk Line Company, Calgary; Mercantile Bank of Canada, Vancouver
1978	Canadian Pacific, London, England; St. Bernadette Church, Surrey, British Columbia

1979	Department of External Affairs, Ottawa; Guaranty Trust, Vancouver; Columbia Trust, Vancouver; Mercantile Bank of Canada, Los Angeles
1980	Crown Life Insurance Company, Vancouver; Daon Development Corporation, Vancouver
1981	Federal Government Building, Calgary; Tricentrol Oils Limited, Calgary; Canadian Industries Limited, Toronto
1982	Children's Hospital, Vancouver
1983	School of Home Economics, University of British Columbia, Vancouver
1983–84	Athabasca University, Athabasca, Alberta
1984	Office of the Prime Minister, Ottawa; Mercantile Bank of Canada, Calgary; Daon Development Corporation, Park Place, Vancouver; St. Matthias Anglican Church, Vancouver
1985	Toronto-Dominion Centre, Toronto

1986	Health Protection Branch, Health and Welfare Canada, Burnaby, British Columbia; Grosvenor International Building, Vancouver
1987	Lloyd's Bank International, Vancouver; Commonwealth Conference, Trade and Convention Centre, Vancouver
1988	Economic Summit, Metropolitan Toronto Convention Centre, Toronto

icheline Beauchemin is an artist who knows no bounds.

She attacks space with the innocent impetuousness of Arachne, the Lydian maiden who dared to challenge the goddess Athena in the art of weaving. After all, has she not already hung from the glass roof of the Québec municipal library a cascade of brushed-aluminum yarns rivalling the majesty of Montmorency Falls? Did she not create the beautiful silvery waves that undulate beneath the immense skylight of Toronto's University Place? It was Micheline too who spread those soaring wings in NOVA Corporation's austere hall in Calgary, making it flicker with orange flames and flash with gold and silver. In Boston, she cut yarns of silk, stainless steel and aluminum to make wings of light for the hall of the Cambridge Center.

After attending the École des beaux-arts de Montréal, Micheline went to Paris to study form with Ossip Zadkine and glassmaking at the École des beaux-arts. From Zadkine she learned the lyrical occupation of space and, from the study of stained-glass making, how light lends magic to glass and to the mirror-like fibres she so often uses.

Micheline calls herself a "painter-weaver", but several of her works, like the one in the Cambridge Center, more closely resemble sculpture. Others are more like mobiles, in constant movement, responding to every current of air. Sometimes she weaves with metallic yarns, creating such works as *Winter*, a gift to the president of France, or *White Totem*, which was given to the wife of the president of Egypt, or *Dark-winged Carapace*, which adorns the Centre industriel et culturel in Paris.

I first met Micheline Beauchemin at Denyse Delrue's. In that narrow gallery located on the mezzanine of an old Victorian house on Crescent Street in Montréal, Micheline was exhibiting some modest crocheted hangings, most of them made from fabric scraps. The next year, in the same gallery, she was showing reversible tapestries. For all practical purposes, these were her last works of moderate dimensions. Nothing or almost nothing she created thereafter could fit within the confines of a gallery. From then on she needed space. Lots of space.

She found it in the Place des Arts in Montréal and the National Arts Centre in Ottawa. There she could use the techniques she had learned in Kyoto, where virtually all the theatre curtains of Japan are made. In the ateliers of Tatsumura, creators of sumptuous obis and kimonos, she studied weaving and coloration, and later on practised the art of tapestry with Kawashima.

Thereafter, Micheline began to seize space even before it was created. By allying herself with the boldest architects, she ensures that they design surfaces in their buildings for her tapestries to occupy or provide spaces in which her huge three-dimensional works will be at home. Give her walls, open cathedrals to her. . . .

There is something quixotic about this woman who soars above life's mundane concerns. She has a charming yet unnerving nonchalance that has led her to set out alone along dangerous routes in India and Cambodia and to venture into politically unstable areas of Peru and Bolivia in search of samples of clothing woven by the Indians. Her imagination is so rich and her nature so generous that she does not hesitate to share her ideas, with both Inuit women in the Arctic and students at the Université du Québec.

From her 300-year-old house at Grondines, Micheline has an unimpeded view of the river. It is here that the Saint Lawrence begins to look less like a river and more like an inland sea. Each day, Micheline looks out over this scene, a vista that is as boundless as her own broad horizons.

Guy Fournier
Writer
Montréal and Paris

Chronology

Born in Longueuil, Quebec
Studied five years at the École des
beaux-arts de Montréal

1952   Draughtsman at Marine Industries,
        Sorel, Quebec

1953   Left for Paris to study drawing at
        the Académie Grande Chaumière
        and stained-glass techniques at the
        École des beaux-arts

1954–55 Travelled in Austria, Germany,
        Switzerland, Spain, North Africa
        and Italy;
        For a year she lived in Greece,
        where she did her first embroideries

1956   Returned to France, where she
        worked at restoring stained-glass
        windows in Chartres

1958   Returned to Canada and worked as
        a costume designer for Radio-
        Canada and for theatres;
        Designed and hooked tapestries
        with rag strips, and made her first
        reversible tapestries

1959   Left Radio-Canada and began to
        work with woollen yarns

1960   Collaborated with architects and
        interior designers to create tapes-
        tries for new buildings

1961   First trip to Japan, where she
        studied weaving techniques for
        theatre curtains and worked with
        Tatsumura in Kyoto;
        Travelled for two months in China
        and Burma

1963   Returned to Montréal; wove a
        tapestry theatre curtain for the
        Place des Arts

1964   Travelled to Mexico, where she
        discovered Indian art

1965   Awarded a scholarship by the
        Canada Council to do research in
        weaving;
        Made a second trip to Japan to
        design the models for a theatre-
        curtain competition being held for
        the Opera of the new National Arts
        Centre in Ottawa; won first prize
        the following year

1966   Returned to Canada, bought a farm
        at Grondines, Quebec, where she
        installed her studio

1967   Made a third trip to Japan, where
        she worked with Kawashima in
        Kyoto;
        Began her first works using silver,
        gold and nylon yarns

1969   Travelled in Cambodia and India

1972   Was the subject of a film showing
        the influence of the St. Lawrence
        River on her tapestries; produced
        by Jean-Marie Drot for Radio-
        Télévision française (Paris) and the
        CBC

1973   Awarded a scholarship by the
        Canada Council to do field research
        in Colombia, Ecuador, Peru and
        Bolivia, documenting and filming
        the clothing woven by the Andes
        and jungle Indians

1974	Member of the Canadian Council of Inuit Arts; made her first trip inside the Arctic Circle to visit the Canadian Inuit
1975	Second trip to Arctic regions; invited by the Canadian Government to teach weaving to Inuit women in Pangnirtung, on Baffin Island
1976	Returned to Grondines, reopened her studio and accepted students from around the world to work with her
1982	Sixth recipient of the Saidye Bronfman Award for Excellence in the Crafts
1985–88	Devoted all her time and energy to defending the St. Lawrence River and its banks against the installation of hydroelectric power lines and pylons; she opposed other projects that would have destroyed the visual beauty as well as the quality of life along the banks of the river in the Grondines area
1988	Resumed her creative work and personal life

Selected Solo Exhibitions

1959	Galerie Denyse Delrue, Montréal
1960	Montreal Museum of Fine Arts, Montréal; Dorothy Cameron Gallery, Toronto
1961	Stratford Festival, Stratford, Ontario; Galerie Delisle, Chicoutimi, Quebec; Here and Now Gallery, Toronto
1962	London Regional Art Gallery, London, Ontario
1966	Sorel Art Centre, Sorel, Quebec
1967	McGill University, School of Architecture, Montréal; Nihon Bashi Gallery, Tokyo
1971	Nova Scotia Festival of the Arts, Halifax; Centre culturel canadien, Paris, retrospective exhibition
1972	Galerie Suzy Langlois, Paris

Selected Group Exhibitions

| 1957 | Palais des beaux-arts, Paris; Musée d'Art moderne, Paris; Canada House, Paris; "First National Fine Crafts Exhibition", National Gallery of Canada, Ottawa; Canadian Pavilion, Brussels World Fair, Belgium |
| 1959 | "Salon de la Jeune Peinture", École des beaux-arts de Montréal; "Exhibit Monsanto", Montreal Museum of Fine Arts, Montréal; Galerie Denyse Delrue, Montréal |

Nordic Wings, the Colour of the Sky
1981
Silk, cotton and rayon threads, acrylic
and nylon filaments, aluminum
Woven, assembled
320 × 247
CMC 88-160 (Bronfman)

1960	"Canadian Artists – Series III", a national travelling exhibition organized by the National Gallery of Canada, Ottawa; Museo de Arte Moderno, Mexico City
1961	O'Keefe Centre, Toronto
1966	"The Wall", McGill University, Faculty of Architecture, Montréal
1967	"Three Hundred Years of Canadian Art", National Gallery of Canada, Ottawa; "Sacred Art", organized by the Ministère des Affaires culturelles, Quebec, for travel to Paris; Youth Pavilion, Expo 67, Montréal; "Good Design of Japan", Tokyo
1970	"Wall Hangings", travelling exhibition organized by the Art Gallery of Ontario, Toronto
1971	Musée d'art contemporain, Montréal
1978	Represented Canada at the International Tapestry Triennial, Lodz, Poland
1980	"Tapestry and Architecture", travelling exhibition in Quebec and Ontario
1981	Represented Canada at the Tenth International Tapestry Biennial, Lausanne, Switzerland; 2e Biennale de tapisserie de Montréal, a travelling exhibition

1982	Musée du Québec, Québec; Terre des Hommes, Montréal; Manoir de Tonnancour, Pointe-du-Lac, Quebec; Galerie Dresdnere, Toronto; "Microcosma", an international travelling exhibition organized by Queen's University, Kingston, Ontario; Galerie Artcurial, Paris
1983	Palacio de Cristal, Madrid
1984	3e Biennale de tapisserie de Montréal, travelled in Canada and Europe; Musée Laurier, Arthabaska, Quebec

Selected Architectural Commissions and Collections

1955	City Hall, Kensington, England
1958	Musée du Québec, Québec; Dorval Airport, Dorval, Quebec
1963	Malton International Airport, Toronto; Salle Wilfrid Pelletier, Place des Arts, Montréal
1964	Alcan Company of Canada, Montréal; Church of Saint-Jean-Vianney, Montréal
1966	National Gallery of Canada, Ottawa

1967	Entrance hall, *Montreal Star* Building, Montréal; Salle Maisonneuve, Place des Arts, Montréal; Le Cercle discothèque in the restaurant Les Ramparts, Montréal	1975–76	Simon Goldberg Conference Centre, Statistics Canada, Ottawa
1968	Queen's Park, Toronto; Opera, National Arts Centre, Ottawa; Canadian Embassy, Tokyo; Quebec House, London; Canada Council Art Bank, Ottawa; Musée du Québec, Québec	1976	Entrance hall, Meridien Hotel, Montréal
		1977	Rideau Hall, Ottawa; City Hall, North York, Ontario; International Airport, San Francisco
		1980	Palais des Congrès, Montréal
		1981	Syntex Inc., Mississauga, Ontario; *Winter*, a tapestry presented to M. François Mitterand, president of France, by the Government of Canada; Vatican Museum, Rome; Entrance hall, NOVA Corporation, Calgary; La Laurentienne, Compagnie d'assurances générales, Québec; Entrance hall, University Place, Toronto
1970	Canada Mortgage and Housing Corporation, Ottawa; Science and Humanities Building, York University, Toronto; Hudson Bay House, Winnipeg; Canadian Pavilion, Expo 70, Osaka, Japan; Province of Quebec Pavilion, Expo 70, Osaka, Japan		
1971	Habitat, Cité du Havre, Montréal	1983	Entrance hall, NOVA Corporation, Calgary; Bibliothèque Gabrielle Roy, Québec
1972	National Defence Building, Ottawa; Right Honourable Pierre Elliott Trudeau, Prime Minister of Canada		
		1984	Civic Centre, Ottawa
1973	Hallmark Center, Kansas City, Kansas	1986–87	Entrance hall, Lavalin Inc., Montréal
1974	Entrance hall, Radio-Canada Building, Montréal	1988	Canadian Museum of Civilization, Samuel and Saidye Bronfman Family Foundation Collection
1975	Inn of the Provinces, Ottawa; Complexe scientifique, Université Laval, Québec		

Homage to the St. Lawrence River 1985
Silk and metallic threads, acrylic fila-
ment
Woven
292 × 145
CMC 86-8 (Bronfman)

Workshops and Lectures

1981	"Formes dans l'architecture", a three-week workshop at the Université du Québec à Chicoutimi
1982	"Tapisserie et architecture", Université du Québec à Trois-Rivières; "Forms in Architecture", Ontario Weavers Association, London, Ontario; "Winter Is My Country", Ontario Weavers Association, London, Ontario; "Tapestry", Ontario Weavers Association, London, Ontario; "Les joies et les douleurs des fibres colorées", Société canadienne des couleurs, Montréal; "Weaving Forms", a one-week workshop at Nipissing University College, North Bay, Ontario

Television

1980	"Visage" for Radio-Québec, produced by Jean Gaétan Séguin
1982	"L'Envers du décor" for Radio-Québec, produced by Marius Théodoresko

Awards and Honours

1957	First prize for stained-glass window, École des beaux-arts, Paris
1959	Province of Quebec prize, Biennale de tapisserie
1960, 1965	Scholarships from the Canada Council
1966	First prize in the tapestry competition for the Opera of the National Arts Centre, Ottawa
1967	Awarded the Governor General's Silver Medal commemorating the Canadian Centennial
1970	Elected Associate Member of the Royal Canadian Academy of Arts
1971	First prize at the tapestry competition, Palais de Justice, Percé, Quebec; Elected Member of the Royal Canadian Academy of Arts
1973	Scholarship from the Canada Council
1974	Appointed Officer of the Order of Canada; Nominated Member of the Canadian Eskimo Arts Council
1976	Awarded the Medal of the Royal Architectural Institute of Canada for her contribution to Canadian and international architecture
1977	Won the competition to design an aluminum mobile for the city hall, North York, Ontario

| 1983 | Recipient of the Prix Philippe-Hébert from the Société Saint-Jean-Baptiste, Montréal; Received an honorary doctorate from the Université Laval, Québec |
| 1988 | Received "La Navette d'Or" [The Golden Shuttle] award from Pierre Desmarais, Montréal, in recognition of the quality and importance of her body of work; Received the Prix d'excellence en arts from the Institut canadien du Québec |

Wayne Ngan

In the pottery of Wayne Ngan we find, perhaps more strongly and consistently than in the work of any other Canadian potter, the presence in form and spirit of Far-Eastern ceramics. That long tradition, which includes Korean and Japanese pottery and in China goes back to the Song dynasty at least, was brought forward into more recent times by such influential practitioners as Hamada and Bernard Leach (who were successful in synthesizing Japanese and English pottery art). It seems appropriate that, as the Canadian who has most fully entered into that tradition, Ngan should live and work on the Pacific Coast and that he should be of Chinese birth.

Wayne Ngan spent his childhood in a Cantonese village, the son of poor parents, who sent him at the age of thirteen or fourteen to live with his grandfather in Vancouver's Chinatown. Defying his grandfather, who had no means of accommodating his grandson's artistic urges or independent spirit, Ngan soon moved off on his own, supporting his attendance at the Vancouver School of Art (from which he graduated in ceramics in 1963) by working nights at a sawmill in a neighbouring municipality. He made his connection with those Far-Eastern artistic sources through books, whose illustrations acquainted him with the forms of various Chinese, Korean and Japanese vessels and with their glazes and decoration. Their influence continues to be expressed in his covered jars, bottles, faceted pots, teabowls, and other pieces. The techniques involved in those

earlier "models" he learned, of necessity, through experimentation.

Today, at the age of fifty-two, Ngan has a firm reputation as a totally committed studio potter, based on the work he has produced over the past twenty years on Hornby Island, one of the Gulf Islands situated between Vancouver Island and the mainland of British Columbia. It is there, too, that he earned his place within the even broader and more ancient company of craftspeople who develop connections, physical and spiritual, that bind their work to a place and time.

Living and working by the sea, in a house and kiln-equipped studio all of his own design and making, he has achieved an integration of his life and his art that embodies the values of simplicity and wholeness at the centre of his personal philosophy. He experiments with the materials that nature offers, incorporating them in his pottery materials or processes. His fondness for clay bodies that are heavy or gritty, forms that are substantial, and glazes or decoration that create texture (such as salt, hakeme, combing, slashing) can be seen as reflections of his continuing impulse to create pottery that asserts the elemental basis of the craft.

There was a dramatic example of Ngan's integrating pattern of thought and action a few years ago when he designed and built his own walk-in wood-fired kiln, whose prototype was the small model of a Song dynasty kiln he had seen in a Beijing museum during a trip to China some ten years earlier and whose image he had carried in his head ever since. For Ngan this slow-burning kiln was a means not only of achieving the softer glazes characteristic of wood-firing but also of sharing more directly in the firing process – that most dramatic and mysterious phase of a pot's creation. Although this kiln fulfilled a long-cherished ambition, it requires many weeks of work to fill, and he continues to use his stoneware, salt-glaze and raku kilns.

Occasionally, when his remoteness from markets becomes frustrating, Ngan threatens to leave his island home, a move that seems unlikely to happen for practical as well as less tangible reasons. Not only has he built himself an enviable facility that would be hard to replace elsewhere but there has been a fusion, into an all-encompassing whole, of work and recreation, inspirational sources and sense of place.

Ngan's holistic approach to art is neither sought after nor capable of realization by most craftspeople today, but his example has the force and persuasiveness of the committed and productive visionary. Out of this commitment have come works that reassert pottery's fundamental meanings while at the same time they echo some of its great moments in time.

Doris Shadbolt
Writer/Curator
North Burnaby, British Columbia

Vase ca. 1970
Stoneware
Hakeme brushwork
23 × 17 diam.
Lent by Ann Mortimer

Vase 1985
Stoneware
Yukon black glaze, brushwork
34 × 23 diam.
CMC 86-165 (Bronfman)

Bottle 1981
Stoneware
Yukon black glaze
49 × 25 diam.
CMC 86-107 (Bronfman)

From left to right:

Teabowl 1986
Stoneware
Local clay, wood-fired
11.4 diam. × 8.5
CMC 86-163 (Bronfman)

Teabowl 1985
Stoneware
Apple ash glaze
12.0 diam. × 8.7
CMC 86-162 (Bronfman)

Teabowl 1985
Stoneware
Oil-spot glaze
11.6 diam. × 9.4
CMC 86-159 (Bronfman)

Teabowl 1985
Stoneware
Oil-spot glaze
12.0 diam. × 8.5
CMC 86-161 (Bronfman)

Teabowl 1985
Stoneware
Victoria glaze
12.3 diam. × 9.0
CMC 86-160 (Bronfman)

Vase 1981
Stoneware
Yukon black glaze
28 × 28 diam.
CMC 86-106 (Bronfman)

Teapot 1985
Stoneware
Yukon black glaze
28 × 26 (including spout)
CMC 86-110 (Bronfman)

Lidded Storage Jar 1985
Stoneware
Salt-glazed (Chinese cobalt)
10 × 10 diam.
CMC 86-164.1–2 (Bronfman)

Lidded Water Jar 1985
Stoneware
Salt-glazed
22 diam. × 18
CMC 85-402.1–2 (Bronfman)

Vase 1981
Stoneware
Salt-glazed
31 × 17 diam.
CMC 86-109 (Bronfman)

Vase 1981
Stoneware
Wood-fired, salt-glazed
32 × 14 diam.
CMC 86-108 (Bronfman)

Vase 1979
Stoneware
Iron slip brushwork, local glaze
28 × 23 diam.
CMC 86-105 (Bronfman)

Lidded Jar 1985
Raku
20 diam. × 15
CMC 86-111.1–2 (Bronfman)

Chronology

1937	Born in Kwantung, China
1951	Immigrated to Canada
1962–63	Entered the Vancouver School of Art, graduating with honours
1965	Studied painting and sculpture in museums, and pottery in antique shops in New York
1965–67	Experimented in painting, sculpture, ceramics and drawing
1968	Studied sculpture, painting and architecture in museums in Paris
1969	Began construction of house, pottery studio and kilns on Hornby Island
1974	Studied and executed bronze sculptures and marble carvings
1975	Received a Canada Council Arts Grant to experiment in raku pottery
1977	Studied Song and early Ming pottery and architecture in Beijing, Xi'an, Fuzhou and Shanghai, China
1978	Worked in Japan with master potter Yoichi Murakami, and travelled with him to pottery centres in Sendai, Kyoto, Kagoshima and Tokyo
1982	Studied sculpture and painting in New York
1983	Seventh recipient of the Saidye Bronfman Award for Excellence in the Crafts; Visited his home village of Kwantung, China, after a 32-year absence; Designed a massive wood kiln inspired by a Song dynasty kiln
1984	Received a Canada Council Art Grant A; Travelled to France to study the paintings of Wassily Kandinsky and Paul Cézanne
1985	Constructed his Song dynasty-inspired wood kiln
1987	Built a small Song dynasty kiln for salt glazes
1988	Sculpted in bronze and painted on pottery; Transformed his pottery studio into a house and his woodshed into a studio

Selected Solo Exhibitions

1965	Bau-Xi Gallery, Vancouver
1970	Art Gallery of Greater Victoria, Victoria
1973–77	House of Ceramics, Vancouver
1974	Potter's Wheel and Gallery, Victoria
1978	Vancouver Art Gallery, Vancouver
1979	Mitsukoshi Department Store, Sendai, Japan
1981	Ontario Crafts Council, Toronto; Rubaiyat Gallery, Calgary
1983	Exhibition of pottery, Taipei, Taiwan; Downstairs Gallery, West Vancouver

Selected Group Exhibitions

1962	"British Columbia Craftsman Exhibition", University of British Columbia, Vancouver; Awarded first prize, Vancouver Art Gallery Purchase Award
1964	"The New Ceramic Presence", University of British Columbia, Fine Arts Gallery
1965	Sculpture exhibition, University of Alberta, Edmonton
1966–67	"Canadian Fine Crafts, 1966–67", National Gallery of Canada, Ottawa
1969	"Canadian Ceramics '69", a national travelling exhibition; awarded first prize, earthenware on raku
1976	"B.C. Ceramics"; awarded first prize, salt-glaze jar
1983	"Pottery Northwest", Montana
1985	"Clay out of the Fire", Pewabic Pottery Gallery, Detroit

Teaching and Workshops

1965–67	Ceramics instructor, Vancouver School of Art, Vancouver
1975–77	Instructor, Shawinigan Summer School of Art, Victoria
1981	Pottery workshop, Montreal Potters' Guild, Montréal
1983	Lecture and workshop at cultural centres in Taipei and Kaohsiung, Taiwan
1981, 1983	Workshops at the Craft Studio, Harbourfront, Toronto
1985	Pottery workshop, Banff School of Fine Arts, Banff, Alberta; Pottery workshop, Edmonton Pottery Guild, University of Alberta, Edmonton
1987	Pottery workshop, Emily Carr College of Art, Vancouver

Television and Video

1980	"Wayne Ngan: Island Potter", produced by Nancy Ryley for the Canadian Broadcasting Corporation
1982	"Reflection of Earth", a video lecture prepared for the Emily Carr College of Art, Vancouver
1983	"Pottery Northwest", a video recording of the opening of his exhibition in Montana
1984	"Seeing Our Way", produced by Al Vitols for the Canadian Broadcasting Corporation

have known Bill Hazzard for quite a few years and would like to mention a few things about this artistic man and his wood carvings. I am a collector of wood carvings – specifically of birds of prey – and, fortunately for me, Bill tends to concentrate his efforts on raptors, that is hawks and owls. I am a hawk and owl bander and therefore have handled hundreds of hawks during migration, when I can really get a close look at these magnificent creatures. Being a stickler for detail, I particularly like Bill's work since he makes the piece "right" – as the carvers say – which means making the bird correct anatomically.

Birds of prey are very difficult to carve. Many carvers have a hard time capturing the fierce and exciting appearance of a raptor. Size is also a problem for many carvers, as can be seen by the variety of shapes and sizes of hawks on display at wood-carving shows. This is probably due to the difficulty in obtaining a mount or study skin, or of actually seeing the raptor up close. But research is probably the most important part of wood carving and Bill Hazzard is very good at this aspect. This means that before Bill even picks up his carving tools he'll spend a lot of time going on field trips, examining study skins in museums and checking photographs to come up with a composition that is unique. By thoroughly researching his project, Bill feels that he can make the carving more lifelike. Bill has told me he "thinks about every bone and feather when carving and what the bird's relationship is to its environment."

I am also involved in the rehabilitation of hawks and owls, and once while Bill was visiting us in Virginia I gave him a Red-tailed Hawk to hold (one that was imprinted and unreleasable). It was a beautiful specimen and you could tell Bill was impressed with the hawk – turning it slowly and feeling its power and seeing up close the beauty and grace of the bird. The bird of prey has a magnificence and nobility that is difficult to capture, particularly with wood. The sculpting can be very tedious, getting the neck, breast, head and beak just right. And the large size of hawks and owls makes Bill's projects major undertakings.

Bill has had no formal instruction in wood carving and came up the hard way – experimenting until he found his own niche. Bill says his object is to "recreate the bird with flow, balance and realism." And by succeeding in this, Bill has come a long way to his present standard of excellence.

Bill puts in some long hours during the long, cold winters in Saskatchewan and he looks forward to a favourite pastime in the spring – fishing. His wife Dorothy and I have kidded Bill occasionally about the length of time he takes on his wood carvings. However, Bill is very meticulous and fights back by saying he can't go any faster. But I'm glad Bill doesn't hurry, since the finished product is a real treasure.

Roger W. Jones
Raptor bander
Falls Church, Virginia

Study for Duck Head and *Demonstra-
tion Block Showing Wood-Burning
Technique* 1985
Basswood
Duck: 13.0 × 8.3 × 5.5
CMC 86-125
Block: 10.8 × 4.0 × 3.9

Chronology

1933	Born in Marlin, Saskatchewan
1940	When his father died, he and his family moved to Bienfait, Saskatchewan
1948	Began working on a farm and in the mines
1958	Moved to Regina and married his wife, Dorothy; Started carving in wood
1959–73	Operated service stations until a knee injury forced him to retire
1973	During a long convalescence, he began refining his wood-carving skills
1976	Entered his first international carving competition, and took home fifteen awards in the Novice class
1984	Eighth recipient of the Saidye Bronfman Award for Excellence in the Crafts
1988–89	Working on a series of songbird carvings

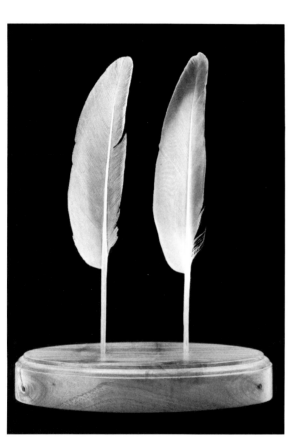

Feather Pair 1985
A Mallard Duck feather mounted with a wooden replica hand-carved by William Hazzard for a competition category that tests the carver's ability to achieve realism (Hazzard's feather is on the left)
Basswood
16.4 × 13.0 × 8.1
CMC 86-100 (Bronfman)

Goshawk with Chipmunk 1985
Basswood, acrylic paint, copper and
brass wire
Sculpted, painted
59 × 45 × 36
CMC 86-98 (Bronfman)

Yellow-headed Blackbirds 1986
Tupelo root, acrylic paint, copper and
brass wire
Sculpted, painted
65 × 35
CMC 86-99 (Bronfman)

Competitions

The World Championship Wildfowl Carving Competitions are held in Maryland; they were formerly at Salisbury but have been at Ocean City since 1979.

1976   *Novice Class*:
Birds of Prey: 1st, 2nd, 3rd
Upland Game: 1st, 3rd
Shorebirds: 1st, 3rd, Honourable Mention
Waterfowl: Honourable Mention
Songbirds: 1st, 2nd, 3rd
1st, 2nd and 3rd place overall in Novice class

1977   *Professional Class* (for this and subsequent competitions):
2 Honourable Mentions

1978   Waterfowl: 1st
Upland Game: 1st
2nd place overall in competition

1979   2 Honourable Mentions

1981   2 Honourable Mentions

1982   Waterfowl: 3rd, Honourable Mention
Judged the Novice class

1983   Birds of Prey: 3rd
Judged the Amateur class

1984   Birds of Prey: 1st, Honourable Mention
2nd place overall in competition
Judged feathers category

1985   Birds of Prey (*Goshawk with Chipmunk*): 1st
1st place overall in competition
Judged duck heads

1986   Birds of Prey: 1st
Judged Amateur class

1987   Shorebirds: 2nd
Birds of Prey: Honourable Mention
2nd place overall in competition
Judged Amateur and Professional classes

Solo Exhibitions

1977   Norman Mackenzie Art Gallery, Regina

1984   Rosemont Art Gallery, Regina

Group Exhibitions

1975   Pacific National Exhibition, Vancouver
Birds of Prey: 1st, 2nd, Bronze Medal

1977   Canadian National Exhibition, Toronto
Open class: 1st

1978   Canadian National Exhibition, Toronto
Upland Game: 1st
Songbirds: 2nd place overall, and Golden Hammer Award;
Saskatchewan Handcraft Festival Juried Exhibition, North Battleford, Saskatchewan: Merit Award, and People's Choice

1979   Saskatchewan Handcraft Festival Juried Exhibition: Merit Award, and People's Choice;

Pacific Flyway Exhibition, Santa Rosa, California: 3 Merit Awards; Dunlop Art Gallery Exhibition, Regina

1980 Saskatchewan Government Insurance Juried Exhibition, Saskatoon: Award of Excellence;
Saskatchewan Handcraft Festival Juried Exhibition, North Battleford: Merit Award;
Saskatchewan Arts Board, Regina: Purchase Award, and People's Choice

1981 Saskatchewan Handcraft Festival Juried Exhibition, North Battleford: Merit Award, and People's Choice

1981–83 "Birds in Art", an exhibition sponsored by Gulf Oil Corporation, which travelled to the Royal Scottish Academy, Edinburgh; the British Museum, London; and the Carnegie Museum, Pittsburgh

1981–88 "Birds in Art", annual exhibition and tour organized by the Leigh Yawkey Woodson Art Museum, Wausau, Wisconsin

1982 Saskatchewan Handcraft Festival Juried Exhibition, North Battleford: Award of Distinction, and People's Choice;
"Transitions", Mendel Art Gallery, Saskatoon, Saskatchewan

1983 Saskatchewan Handcraft Festival Juried Exhibition, North Battleford: People's Choice

1985 Two-person exhibition, Joe Moran Gallery, Regina

1987 Ducks Unlimited and World Wildlife Fund Art Auction

Selected Collections

Canadian Museum of Civilization, Samuel and Saidye Bronfman Family Foundation Collection

James Art Gallery, Saskatoon, Saskatchewan

Leigh Yawkey Woodson Art Museum, Wausau, Wisconsin

Saskatchewan Arts Board, Regina

Saskatchewan Museum of Natural History, Regina

Saskatchewan Telecommunications, Regina

Weyburn Arts Council, Weyburn, Saskatchewan

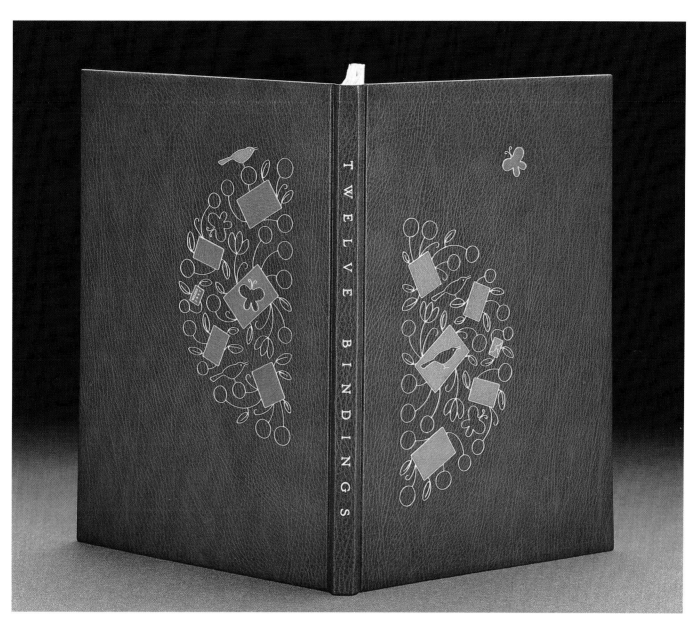

Binding for "Twelve Bindings: Michael Wilcox" 1987
Nigerian goatskin
Onlays blocked and tooled in gold, silk board-linings, gilded and goffered edges
35.6 × 25.0 × 1.3
CMC 87-80 (Bronfman)

*M*ost of the arts and crafts are concerned with excellence in a single medium, such as wood, clay, metal, fabric, leather, each requiring a particular aptitude. However, fine bookbinding as we know it on this continent is a multimedia craft, demonstrating skill in the use of a variety of materials and the techniques for wedding them into a consummate whole. Through the centuries, books have been bound with covers of elaborately carved wood, intricate metalwork and handwoven fabrics, besides the traditional fine leatherwork featuring onlays, decorative gold tooling or jewel inlays. Of course, these bindings are often the product of a cooperative effort by different craftsmen, but many bookbinders have developed skills in other craft media to produce complex bindings by themselves. When a master bookbinder is also a gifted artist, we have what is known in modern terms as a designer/bookbinder, the ultimate goal of those who practise the craft.

When Michael Wilcox first came to my door on 5 September 1962, he had just finished a full apprenticeship in fine binding at George Bayntun's of Bath, one of the last of the prestigious bookbinding establishments in England. As he was already skilled in the rudiments of fine binding, I was more than happy to give him part-time work for a few months until his job at the Royal Ontario Museum was ready. We found instant rapport in our shared interest in art and nature, books and bookbinding. Our relationship was a mutual exchange of ideas and inspiration, through which I like to think we both increased in stature.

Michael's work as preparator in the Mammalogy Department of the Museum ended when he discovered that advancement would not be possible without many years of academic study. This interlude was not wasted, however, as it proved to be one of the fallow periods in life that are sometimes necessary for real growth. And he did win one special bonus for the time he spent there – his wife Suzanne Stark, an amateur naturalist and weaver who was also on the staff. It was near her family home north of Burleigh Falls, Ontario, that they purchased eleven acres of Canadian Shield woodland with an attractive cottage and separate shop for a bindery. Here, in the solitude they both love, close to the highway but bordered on three sides by unbroken wilderness, with birds, a beaver pond and occasional bear and deer, he has continued with his book arts, honing the skills he had and acquiring new ones. He taught himself metal engraving and made his own brass tools for tooling gold, including complete sets of the alphabet for titling book covers. Whatever equipment he could not find or afford to buy he has improvised.

The process of leather onlay decoration is one of the most advanced and difficult arts of fine binding, and few binders develop the confidence that comes from a combination of skill, patience and artistic perception to do much serious work. Michael's fertile imagination and sense of design, along with his skill in gold tooling, have produced work that compares favourably with that of the finest binders anywhere, past or present. Some of his illusory, three-dimensional work with "shaded" gold tooling over coloured onlays is breathtaking.

Michael's work seems to me to be more expressive of the subject matter of the book and the mood of the author than it is a stereotyped signature of the craftsman, or of a certain period style. This is as it should be if an artist is to be sensitive to his material and not limited by technical possibilities. I find Mike's work intuitive, spontaneous and rarely inhibited by any kind of academic restraint. Indeed, some book collectors, who are perhaps the final jury, give him a place among the best designer/bookbinders in the Western world today.

Robert Muma
Artist and retired bookbinder
Toronto

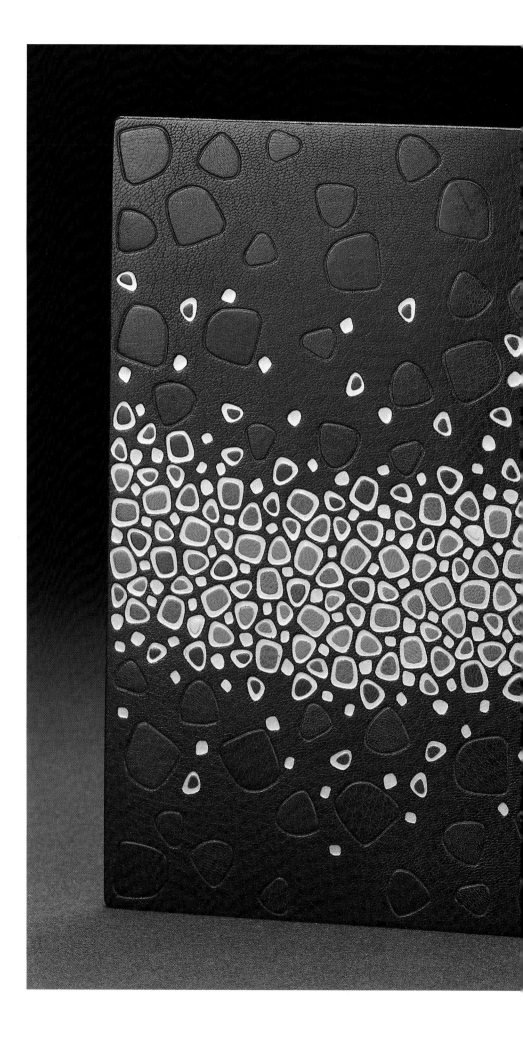

Binding for "Klondike", by Pierre Berton
1986
Nigerian goatskin
Inlays and onlays tooled in gold and
blind, leather doublures, silk flyleaves,
gilded and goffered edges
27.3 × 18.9 × 6.5
CMC 86-150
Gift of Pierre Berton

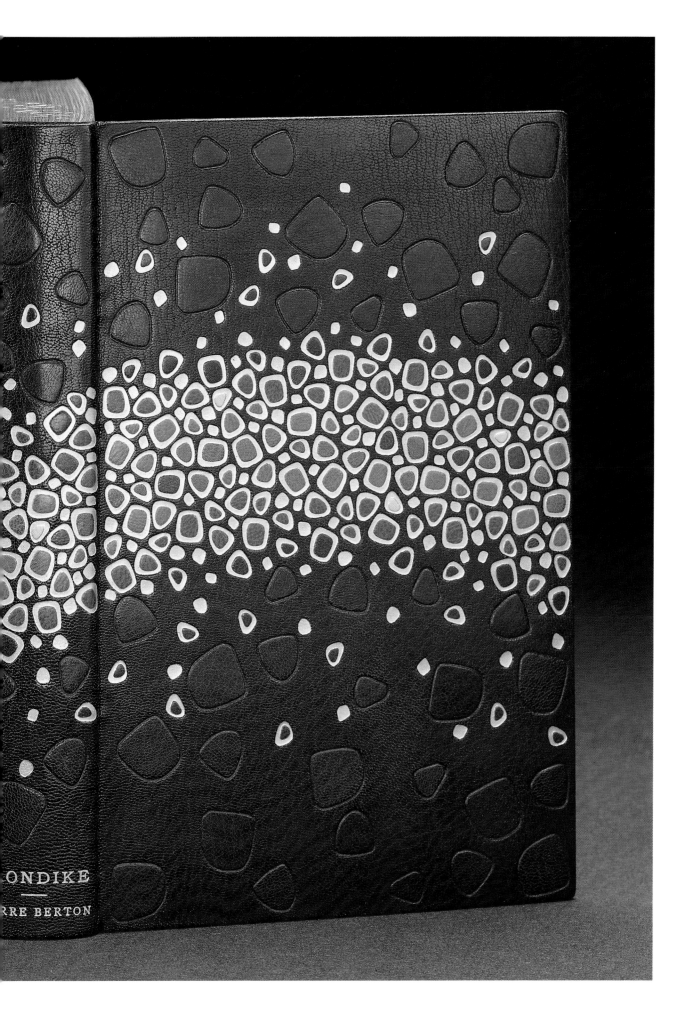

Chronology

1939	Born in Bristol, England
1955	Began a six-year apprenticeship in bookbinding with Edward Everard, Printer, of Bristol; Began five years of study as a part-time student in the department of printing, Bristol College of Technology
1960	Gained the City and Guilds of London Final Certificate in General Bookbinding; Apprenticeship transferred to George Bayntun, bookbinder and bookseller of Bath
1961	Completed his apprenticeship and returned to Bristol to work as a journeyman binder with W.H. Ware and Sons, general bookbinders; Began evening classes in bookbinding and life drawing at the Bristol College of Art
1962	Emigrated to Canada and worked at various temporary binding jobs
1963	Worked for six months on book restoration with Robert Muma, bookbinder and leather craftsman of Toronto; Joined the staff of the Royal Ontario Museum, Toronto, as a technician for the Department of Mammalogy
1967	Left the Royal Ontario Museum and moved to the Kawartha Lakes, Ontario, as a storekeeper
1969	Set up a one-man studio to bind books for antiquarians, dealers, collectors and libraries
1976	Began a five-year project with the Thomas Fisher Rare Book Library, University of Toronto, restoring a collection of early medical books
1981	Completed the University of Toronto contract and began working exclusively on commissions for fine bindings
1985	Ninth recipient of the Saidye Bronfman Award for Excellence in the Crafts
1989	Continues to work exclusively on commissions for fine bindings

Solo Exhibition

1983	Thomas J. Watson Library, Metropolitan Museum of Art, New York

Selected Group Exhibitions

1978	"Hand Bookbinding Today, an International Art", San Francisco Museum of Modern Art, San Francisco; "Reader, Lover of Books, Lover of Heaven", North York Public Library, Willowdale, Ontario

1979 "The Tradition of Fine Book-binding in the Twentieth Century", Carnegie-Mellon University, Pittsburgh, Pennsylvania

1980 "Bookbinding: A Living Art", Museum of Fine Arts, Houston, Texas

1981 "Reader, Lover of Books", North York Public Library, Willowdale, Ontario;
"The Guild of Book Workers: 75th Anniversary Exhibition", Grolier Club, New York

1982 "20th-Century Bookbinding", Art Gallery of Hamilton, Hamilton, Ontario

1984 "Horizons in Bookbinding", Brighton Polytechnic Gallery, Brighton, England

1987 "Book Arts", Brampton Public Library and Art Gallery, Brampton, Ontario

Publications

1983 "Binding the Pennyroyal Press *Alice*", *Fine Print* (San Francisco), October 1983, p. 168

1985 *Twelve Bindings: Michael Wilcox* (Austin, Texas: W. Thomas Taylor)

Lectures and Workshops

1984 Demonstrator for the Guild of Book Workers' third seminar on standards of excellence in hand bookbinding, Pittsburgh, Pennsylvania

1985 Demonstrator for the Guild of Book Workers' fourth seminar on standards of excellence in hand bookbinding, San Francisco

1986 Bookbinding workshop and lecture, Arts of the Book Exhibition, Vancouver

1987 Lecture and slide presentation to the William Morris Society of Canada at University College, University of Toronto, Toronto

Brooch with Eagle Design 1970
22-carat gold, abalone
Constructed, repoussé, set
7.0 × 5.0
Lent by M. Joan Chalmers, C.M.

What sort of an artist is Bill Reid? Sculptor, carver, jeweller, printmaker – all of these, and poet also. Few great artists are witty, fewer still are gifted wordsmiths. For Bill, words are like the gold and the cedar he works into the forms of myth, history and imagination.

In his art he is indebted to a variety of sources, and many artists are indebted to him. He works eclectically, learning techniques where he chooses and acquiring knowledge from other artists, from galleries, museums and libraries. He studied the making of jewellery at the Ryerson Institute of Technology, Toronto, spent time with Mungo Martin when the old carver resumed working in the last years of his life, and worked with scholars and artists whose talents and knowledge complemented his own. His mastery gained from so many sources, he was confined to none and could work freely and creatively with different traditions. Undoubtedly the traditions of Haida art are closest to him, but the conventions of Haida and other Northwest Coast sculpture were constantly expanding and Bill has further enriched them.

His studios – the various spaces where shavings and plaster dust mingle – attract helpers who become learners and sometimes significant artists themselves, whose jewellery, sculpture and prints are recognized as creatively different from those of their master. Bill is not an indulgent teacher. Pupils sink or swim as they choose, the teacher sparing of praise and words of guidance. What need is there for praise and guidance when he shows by his own past and present work what must be done?

Earlier Northwest Coast art had humour, at times strong, mocking and satiric, at others embodying a sense of pure fun. Wit and the sense of fun died as the art itself dwindled to reflect tourist demands. Bill has revived the humour; his is sometimes gentle but often robust. He has absorbed the standard works of scholarship, and, although no copyist, he has studied the art of the region in museum collections all over the world. He has written and spoken widely as an analyst of Northwest Coast art and as a poet celebrating its beauty.

The major strengths of traditional Northwest Coast art lay in sculpture and oratory. In his sculpture and in his jewellery, Bill has given new forms to the myth and a different expression to the wit. His spoken word is no less strong for the absence of oratorical noise and flourish, and his written word matches the oratory of the past.

Bill is an artist extraordinary.

Harry Hawthorn
Emeritus professor of anthropology
University of British Columbia
Vancouver

Chronology

1920	Born in Victoria; mother, Sophie Reid (née Gladstone), Haida of Skidegate, Queen Charlotte Islands; father, American
1940	Discovered his relationship to Haida art and culture
1943	First visit as an adult to the Charlottes; spent time with his grandfather, Charles Gladstone, nephew and heir to Charles Edenshaw, last of the great traditional Haida artists
1948	Enrolled in jewellery courses at the Ryerson Polytechnic Institute, Toronto
1951	After his apprenticeship at a platinum and diamond shop, Reid returned to Vancouver, where he continued to work as a broadcaster for the Canadian Broadcasting Corporation until 1958; Set up a basement workshop for jewellery making
1952	Inspired by examples of traditionally crafted Haida silver bracelets, Reid began to produce jewellery in the style of his Haida ancestors
1957	With the late Mungo Martin, Reid spent two weeks carving a small figure on a copy of a Haida totem pole (now installed near the Peace Arch on the Canada–United States border at Blaine, Washington)
1965–66	Worked as a consultant on "Arts of the Raven", a major exhibition celebrating Canada's Centennial, at the Vancouver Art Gallery, Vancouver
1967	Produced his first gold box, fabricated from 22-carat gold sheet, carved and engraved, with lid featuring a three-dimensional eagle
1968	Received a Canada Council Senior Grant to study European and Northwest Coast collections and to improve his gold- and silver-smithing techniques at the Central School of Modern Design in London
1972	After his return to Canada and a three-year work period in Montréal, Reid re-established his Vancouver workshop
1974	Retrospective exhibition at the Vancouver Art Gallery, Vancouver
1976–78	Designed and carved a traditional Haida totem pole for his mother's village of Skidegate, Queen Charlotte Islands, with assistants Gary Edenshaw, Joe David and Robert Davidson

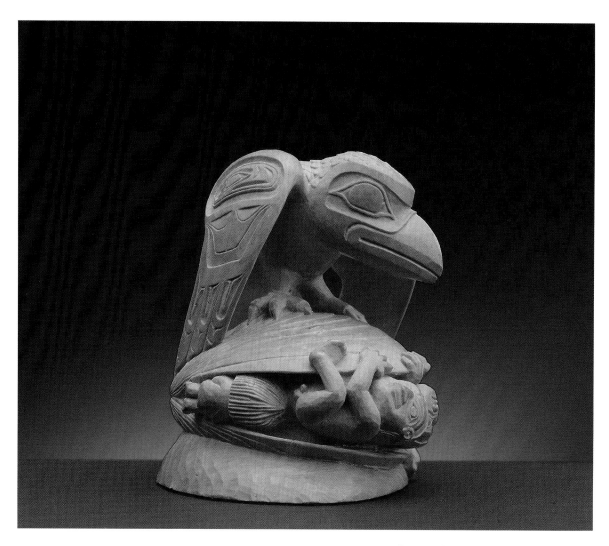

Raven Discovering Mankind in a Clam-shell 1970
Boxwood
Carved
7.0 × 6.9 × 5.5
Lent by the Museum of Anthropology, University of British Columbia, Vancouver

*Box with Beaver and Human Design,
and Killer Whale on Lid* 1970
22-carat gold
Repoussé, chased, cast, constructed
9.9 × 9.0 × 7.9
Lent by the Royal British Columbia
Museum, Victoria

1986	Tenth recipient of the Saidye Bronfman Award for Excellence in the Crafts; Retrospective exhibition, "Bill Reid: Beyond the Essential Form", held at the Museum of Anthropology, University of British Columbia; "Retrospective photographique", held at the Galerie Mansart, Paris

Selected Large-Scale Commissions

1958–62	Invited by Harry Hawthorn, head of the anthropology department at the University of British Columbia, to create a section of a Haida village (two houses and attendant totem poles) for a display at the university
1968	British Columbia Provincial Museum, Victoria
1972, 1987	Canadian Museum of Civilization (formerly the National Museum of Man)
1980–83	Designed and directed the construction of *Raven and the First Men*, a yellow-cedar sculpture commissioned by the Museum of Anthropology, University of British Columbia, Vancouver
1983–84	Designed the large-scale *Killer Whale*, a bronze sculpture commissioned by the Vancouver Public Aquarium, Stanley Park, Vancouver
1983–86	Designed and constructed two dugout cedar canoes measuring 7.3 and 15 metres long, using traditional Haida building techniques; they were commissioned by the Bank of British Columbia for Expo 86
1984–85	Designed the large-scale *Mythic Messengers*, a bronze mural, commissioned by Teleglobe Canada, Burnaby, British Columbia; Westcoast Transmission Company, Vancouver
1985	Carved and installed *Phyllidula, the Shape of Frogs to Come* in the Vancouver Art Gallery
1986	Awarded the contract to design a large bronze sculpture for the new Canadian chancery in Washington, D.C.

Selected Publications

1967	"The Art – An Appreciation", in *Arts of the Raven* (Vancouver: Vancouver Art Gallery)
1971	*Out of the Silence*, photography by Adelaide de Menil (Fort Worth, Texas: Amon Carter Museum)
1975	*Form and Freedom*, a dialogue on Northwest Coast Indian art with Bill Holm (Rice University, Houston, Texas: Institute for the Arts)
1976	"Eulogy to Wilson Duff", *Vanguard* 5, no. 8: 13–14; reprinted in *The World Is As Sharp As a Knife*, edited by Donald Abbott (Vancouver: University of British Columbia Press, 1977)

1983	Foreword and illustrations for *Monumental Art: Villages of the Queen Charlotte Islands*, by George F. MacDonald (Vancouver: University of British Columbia Press)
1984	*The Raven Steals the Light*, stories by Bill Reid and Robert Bringhurst, drawings by Bill Reid (Vancouver and Toronto: Douglas & McIntyre); "These Shining Islands", in *Island at the Edge*: Part I, *The Legacy of Change* (Vancouver and Toronto: Douglas & McIntyre for the Islands Protection Society)
1985	"The Anthropologist and the Article", *Culture* 4, no. 2: 63–65

Television and Films

1956	"People of the Potlatch", script and narration by Bill Reid, produced by Gene Lawrence for the Canadian Broadcasting Corporation
1963	"Totems", script and narration by Bill Reid, produced by Gene Lawrence for the CBC
1978	*Bill Reid*, produced by Jack Long for the National Film Board of Canada
1980	"Bill Reid", produced by Jennifer Hodge for the CBC
1984	*A Day in the Life of a Parkinsonian*, produced by Sandoz Canada Inc.

1986	"Song of the Haida Canoe", produced by Chris Wootten for the CBC
1988–89	"Loota: Journey Home", produced by Nina Wisnicki for the CBC

Honours and Awards

1977	Molson Award, given by the Canada Council for cultural achievement
1979	Diplôme d'Honneur, Canadian Conference of the Arts, for service to the arts
1985	Fellowship, Ryerson Polytechnical Institute; Bill Reid Day, City of Vancouver
1987	Life Achievement Award, City of Vancouver
1988	Freeman of the City of Vancouver, in honour of lifetime achievement

Honorary LL.D. Degrees

1976	University of British Columbia, Vancouver; Trent University, Peterborough, Ontario
1978	York University, Toronto
1979	University of Victoria, Victoria
1983	University of Western Ontario, London, Ontario

Necklace 1972
Silver
Fabricated
53.0 × 6.5
Lent by the Ontario Crafts Council,
Toronto

Lidded Box with Bear Design 1985–86
Silver, leather lining
Chased, constructed
11.8 × 8.8 × 5.5
CMC 86-41.1–2
Massey Foundation Collection

Photograph Credits

page

12 Courtesy Robin Hopper

16 *Top:* Collection of the Lilly Library, Indiana University; courtesy Michael Wilcox
    Bottom: Collection of the Humanities Research Center, University of Texas at Austin; courtesy Michael Wilcox

17 Collection of the Canadian Museum of Civilization; photograph by Rolph Bettner

18 Courtesy City of Ottawa Archives, *Ottawa Journal* Collection; photograph by Russell Mant

19 Photograph by Eric Betteridge

21 *Left:* Collection of the Canadian Museum of Civilization; photograph by Larry Raynard
    Right: Courtesy William Hazzard; photograph by Tom H. Johnson

22, Courtesy Monique Cliche-Spénard; photo-
23 graph at lower right by Luce Bernard

24, Courtesy Micheline Beauchemin; photograph
25 on page 25 by George C. Fenyon

26 Courtesy Micheline Beauchemin; photograph by McKay, Toronto

27, Courtesy Wayne Ngan; photograph on
28 page 28 by Bob Cain

29 Courtesy Robin Hopper; photograph on the left from the *Reading Times* and on the right from the *Barrie Examiner*

30 Courtesy Robin Hopper; photograph by Jim Ryan

31 Courtesy Joanna Staniszkis

32 Courtesy Toronto-Dominion Centre, Toronto

33 Courtesy Doucet–Saito; photograph at top left by Shoichi Koinuma, and the other two by Raymond Martinot

34 Courtesy Bill Reid

35 Courtesy University of British Columbia, Museum of Anthropology, Bill Reid Archives

Portraits
All the colour portraits are from the collection of the Canadian Museum of Civilization (photographs by Rolph Bettner) except the following:

74 Courtesy Doucet–Saito; photograph by Jean-François Ozoux

94 Courtesy Micheline Beauchemin; photograph by Kedl of Québec

Artifacts
Except for the following, all the photographs of the works of craft are by Harry Foster of the Canadian Museum of Civilization and are in the Museum's collection

75– Courtesy Doucet–Saito; the photographs on
79 pages 75, 78 and 79 are by Raymond Martinot, the one at the top of page 77 is by Claire Dufour, and the others on pages 76 and 77 are by Jean-Pierre Beaudin

Hallmarks
Collection of the Canadian Museum of Civilization; photographs by Richard Garner

Coordinating editor
Viviane Appleton

Design
Eiko Emori Inc.

Typesetting
The Runge Press Limited

Colour separations
Running and Ojala Inc.

Printing
M.O.M. Printing